HOW TO BE A FUCKING UNICORN

HOW TO BE A FUCKING UNICORN

A guide to living your best life,
as your TRUE SELF.
In a world where you are told
to fit in, STAND OUT.

LEAH LUNA LIGHTWARRIOR

First Edition Published by Leah Luna Lightwarrior

Copyright ©2018 Leah Luna Lightwarrior

Edited and formatted by WOW Book Publishing™

ISBN 978-1-9995845-0-4

CONTENTS

About The Author vii

Foreword...ix

Why You Should Read This Book xi

My Journey To Becoming A "Unicorn"................... xiii

Perspective Of Life xxi

1. Live Now 1

2. Love Yourself First 12

3. Your Vibe Attracts Your Tribe............................25

4. Release Your Inner Child....................................33

5. Be, Before You Do...40

6. You Create Your Reality 50

7. Go Your Own Way...60

8. Re-Programme Yourself.......................................77

9. Give, Not To Receive 89

10. Follow Your Dreams..95

11. Enjoy Your Journey... 107

Acknowledgements 115

ABOUT THE AUTHOR

Leah-Brooklyn A.K.A Leah Luna is passionate and dedicated to living a life from her soul. She doesn't identify by any labels, she sees herself as a soul on a journey as a human, and a "Lightwarrior" here to shine her light to guide others to their own; to help others live to their fullest potential and love who they are. She has always had the mindset of following her dreams and determination to never give up and help others do the same. She feels a pull to be her greatest self, to be of service to others, and to help them be their greatest selves.

Leah-Brooklyn is a singer, creator of a clothing movement '11.11 Earth', animal activist, inspirational speaker, spiritual social media influencer, blogger and vlogger.

FOREWORD

by the Author

This is for the misfits, the dreamers, the 'crazy ones'; the people that want more for their life than "average". I used to try and fit in, try to dull my shine, be like everyone else. I've always felt different, I wondered why I wasn't like everyone else and didn't want to do what others told me to do.

But now I LOVE who I am. I LOVE being "weird". I LOVE BEING MYSELF. I want to help YOU be yourself too. Truly express yourself, follow YOUR dreams, live YOUR life to the fullest, being true to yourself and not giving a fuck what anyone thinks.

THIS IS YOUR LIFE.

We all deserve to live our greatest lives and be free to be who we truly are.

I am writing this book as I feel a mission to help others find and love themselves, to be able to live their greatest life. Everyone deserves to follow their dreams and love every moment of their time here on Earth.

I long for a world where we can all live in harmony and be guided by love.

I believe changing the world starts with changing yourself.

Of everything I feel I could write about, I believe self-love and being the greatest you is the most important. It is through loving and being true to yourself that you can truly love others, feel free and live your best life.

Being your greatest self is the greatest gift you can give to the world.

IT'S TIME TO BE YOU.

It's time to fulfil your true potential.

ARE YOU READY TO BE A FUCKING UNICORN?!

UNICORN - *Metaphor-* An extraordinary, other worldly being that stands out from the crowd, someone who knows who they are, love themselves and exudes MAGIC a.k.a YOUR TRUE SELF.

WHY YOU SHOULD READ THIS BOOK

"Leah-Brooklyn's magical words are so incredibly inspiring and motivating. Her positivity is passed on to those who are blessed enough to connect with her story. Her love for life is clear and she is an inspiration to others."

—Danielle, Teacher

"Leah-Brooklyn is a true bright and strong ray of light! I am thankful for her presence, she radiates light to my life with her posts on IG. She is so amazing and inspiring. Her light grows by the day and humanities consciousness is on the rise with people like her! She reminds me of the greatest self-love within and how it helps [harmonise] everything when we are our greatest self. She is truly inspirational!"

—Tomer, Yoga Teacher and Musician

"Leah-Brooklyn's debut book is a true masterpiece, she has condensed the most valuable and practical knowledge she has gained from her own personal transformation, into a step by step to releasing the unique, infinite being within, causing a cascade of positivity to flow in every area of your life."

—Nathan Woodruffe,
Author and Tiny House Creator

"Leah-Brooklyn is a creative individual with an innovative outlook on self-acceptance and confidence. Leah's modern spiritual advice has been a great influence for not only me, but her thousands of dedicated followers. As a friend, I am bursting with pride to witness Leah-Brooklyn excel in helping others mentally unleash their best possible version of their self. I have no doubt that Leah will bring out self-love, acceptance and confidence in others, just like she has done for me"

—Amy Walker, Artist

"How often do you meet people in life and think "f*cking WOW"? You see this person with a ring of light around them, like goodness is emanating from them. You appreciate they have wisdom beyond the confines of this beautiful planet. This is exactly what I thought when I met Leah-Brooklyn. Leah is a true believer in the fact we create our reality, therefore we can make our dreams come alive and that is exactly what she is teaching us in this inspiring book! Get ready for a game changer!"

—Laura Maginess, Blogger at pinktartandoll.com
and Founder of GLASGLOW GIRLS CLUB

MY JOURNEY TO BECOMING A "UNICORN"

I didn't fit in. I felt like I had to, I was surrounded by it so I thought I must become it, like everyone else. Because it's "normal" right? I changed who I truly was. I pretended so others would like me, so I "fit in". I lived an act. I always knew something didn't add up about the way society lived. Why were we born on to this planet just to go to school, get a job, have a family, "settle down" and then die? For what? What is the point in that? I always wanted more. I knew I had my dreams for a reason. Why would I be so passionate about something and feel it so strongly within myself, if I was just to ignore it and do what everyone else did?

I saw there were other humans who had achieved greatness in their lives and I was going to be one of them. It's safe to say my big dreams were not understood by those around me.

"You'll never achieve that", "You have pipe dreams that will never come true, Leah-Brooklyn, and you'll be like everyone else", "Who do you think you are?!"

Statements of doubt and criticism came from "friends", teachers, others my age, online bullies and even people that were closest to me. That's something to understand about seeing life differently from others, you will always face doubt, criticism, and questions. It's rare for people to do something outside of the "norm". People have become limited in beliefs of what is possible for their lives, so they have accepted what they think is true and, sadly, a lot of people settle in their lives instead of going after what their hearts truly want. They have been taken over by fear. It takes true courage to follow your heart.

I spent my teenage years and first couple of years of my 20's trying to fit in, trying to be accepted, not being my truest, greatest self. I was rejected most of my school years and felt like a true misfit. I was in relationships from the age of 16 until 20, because I was rejected by boys in school, and I just wanted to be loved. I wanted that fairytale relationship like I saw in the movies, I thought that was true happiness. I did not realise how important it is to love myself and know myself first before I can love someone else and be with the right soul for me. I didn't know who I was, I didn't love myself, but I didn't know that I didn't. I thought I was me. I then tried to fit in again and had a "partying" stage, I had friends that weren't really my friends, I slept with boys that didn't love me, I did things that I didn't really want to do; I just wanted to be accepted and loved. I worked in a job that I wasn't happy in. I ate junk food, I did squats so my bum was bigger and guys fancied me. I didn't have any sense of individuality. I wanted to be like a celebrity, I followed their lives and bought their products. I followed trends, I saved up to have designer clothes so that I felt cool and important. I lived my live looking forward to holidays and just putting up with all the days before them and spending time miserable after them, just waiting for the next trip. I didn't think I was lost, but I was.

It wasn't until I hit the lowest point, the most painful rejection from a man that I was mesmerised by, that I was able to find who I truly was. I was suicidal, every day of life was a drag, I felt so much pain in my body, my head was working overtime just thinking about him constantly, I put on a lot of weight because I was eating so much junk to comfort my pain. I drank bottles of vodka (I've never been a drinker) and got shitfaced and lay on the floor listening to a playlist of songs that reminded me of him. I didn't feel like life was worth living without him. I had panic attacks, I would hit the ground and scream and punch and cry. I felt like I didn't know anything about myself anymore, I didn't know who I was. I didn't know what to do. Every day was full of darkness, it was horrendous. I needed help, I was so close to taking anti-depressants and seeing a psychiatrist because my mum was so scared and we didn't know what to do.

But from my darkest pain, from going insane and feeling completely broken and a shadow of myself, an incredible journey started. I started to help myself, through seeking truth about life, who I really am, why we are really here, what the purpose is of all of this and how I live MY purpose on this crazy planet.

Before I met the guy, I discovered and started putting into practise "The Law of Attraction". I found out about this through listening to the audio book of "The Secret". In the beginning, when my mum used to play it in the car I would think "What a lot of absolute bullshit". I was used to my mum going through "crazy phases" of different ways of seeking truth, buying different books, trying new things, we tried it all! I just thought "Here we go again!" Because to me, I didn't really wanna know "the meaning of life", I thought it was boring and something your R.E teacher in school would try and make you think about. I just wanted to listen to music, go shopping and go on holiday! I mean really, we are all on this planet, don't really have a clue why we are here and we are all seeking answers to the meaning of all of this, whether we ignore it or not, we all have our own truth to find of why we are here. Some people can spend their whole lifetime just "tiptoeing through life hoping to make it safely to death" and not actually truly living for a purpose. In fact, to this day, I can tell someone that "I'm living my purpose" and they will think I'm crazy, and that's crazy to me now! We ALL have a purpose here! We're not here for no reason, no matter what you believe in!

Anyway, one day I started to actually listen to "The Secret" and thought *wow*. I actually started to use it, and it WORKED! I had really discovered the true power we all have and just wanted to tell everyone! And of course, a lot of people just thought I was crazy! So I kept it to myself, and got "What you think, you become", a Buddha quote tattooed on me to remind me of the power of the Law of Attraction.

So when I was trying to pull myself out of my depression, I remembered this, and also when I went to New York, the guy I fell for, had passed on so much knowledge to me one night when we were at a bar. I mean, I was a little drunk and I did think he was a little crazy but I loved it and I believed everything he said, it resonated with me like I was remembering what I already knew within (which I was), and it made me fall for him even more. He was teaching me incredible things that I never knew at that time, if that's not a complete turn on I don't know what is! Some of the things he mentioned to me, things that happen in the world that I knew the truth about and just ignored because "it didn't concern me", he was bringing these things up and I was realising just how important they were. I didn't do anything with the knowledge at first because I was too busy thinking about him, but one day my mum mentioned something that he had actually mentioned to me and we were always interested in, so we started to research. From starting this research it lead us to so much truth that we didn't stop seeking! I read so many incredible, life-changing books. I learned from amazing teachers and started to actually find out who I am and why I am here.

I started shedding the "old self", who I used to be and all the things I was taught to believe, or things I had picked up from other people that wasn't who I am. I discovered my true purpose and started to live from my soul, realising we are all souls in human bodies for a temporary amount of time, and we are all one. All the labels that separate us aren't real. I realised that LOVE is the answer and truly started living as who I really am. I found connection to nature and animals, I found the true magic in life, and saw the illusions that distract us from finding our true purpose.

I started to feel a true calling to help the planet be a better place with my life, through the things that I love, from living my truth, my purpose, living from my SOUL. Beyond labels. Beyond illusions of limitation. I discovered the true power that was within me all along that just had to be tapped into.

Every day is a journey of evolving, of learning. It's incredible. The way I see life now compared to the way I used to see life is unbelievable.

I live life from my soul, from the answers and power I have within, the true power we ALL have within. I remembered that I am a "Lightworker" and I am here to guide the planet to love and peace. I am a part of a team of souls who decided to come to Earth at this time.

I now live my life in service to the higher power, the planet and all its beings. I live from LOVE and not fear.

And discovering my true power and the true potential we all hold, has lead me to writing this book. I believe we all have the power to make a difference in this world, and to do that we have to live our greatest lives our true potential, our purpose.

When I discovered who I was, I felt MAGICAL, out of this world, limitless, and FREE. Like a Unicorn.

In this book I share stories and truths I have learned along my journey that have truly helped me change my life and live my greatest potential and true purpose. I want to help others do the same!

This book is based on my own experiences and lessons, and also the books I've read, and teachers I've learned from. We are all one so when another human being shares knowledge and we resonate with it, they are reminding us of something we have forgotten, that's what I want to help you do. Just as great teachers like Tony Robbins, Don Miguel Ruiz and Abraham Hicks have guided me to.

What is written in this book has the potential to truly change your life in the most amazing way, but you can't just read the book, you actually have to take action!

It's easy to listen to information and know its true, but if you don't take action, nothing will change and you will stay stuck in the same patterns and ways of thinking that is currently keeping you from living your best life.

The choice is yours.

Are you ready to be a fucking Unicorn?!

PEACE, LOVE AND LIGHT

Leah Luna Lightwarrior

PERSPECTIVE OF LIFE

One day you won't be here. Your time on this planet as a human being is temporary.

How do you want to spend your time here?

Does everything you stress over really matter when you consider just how small you are in comparison to the Universe?

Or just how short your time is here in comparison to the history of humanity?

Days are only going to keep passing by, you are only going to keep getting older, and it can't be stopped.

So do you want to 'tip toe' through life, hoping to make it 'safely' to death?

Or do you want to TRULY LIVE while you're here and ENJOY your time on Earth?

Death is inevitable, it shouldn't be feared. From the moment we were born it was already destined that one day we will die too, and who knows when that day will be?

Personally, I believe we are all energy and energy can never die, only transform, and that's what I believe we will do. Who really knows?

All we really know is that we know nothing. We will never know all of the answers.

What we do know is that we have power over how we choose to live our lives while we are here. Your time here is temporary, it is precious so use it wisely. Time is the only thing we can't get back.

We were born as MIRACLES. At what point did we forget that? Our bodies are incredible miracles. We breathe without thinking about it, our hearts beat, our cells renew.

So when did we forget "miracles" are possible in every area of our lives.

When did we settle for less than what we truly want or deserve?

It's time to take back your power and DECIDE to live your best life!

LIVE NOW

STOP WAITING FOR HAPPINESS

It's time to stop waiting for happiness. "Oh I'll be happy when I lose weight" or "I'll be happy at the weekend", or "I'll be happy when I go on holiday!"

Realise this, life is happening NOW. Waiting for happiness is going to lead to disappointment. Happiness doesn't just happen to you, you have to consciously choose to be happy, and you CAN be happy NOW!

Think of how many days of your precious life would be wasted if you were only happy at the weekend, 261 days every year of 'unhappiness' simply because you decided that Monday—Friday are days of average, 'every day' life. Realise, every day is the same. The sun rises and sets. Days are just defined by labels, and people have been conditioned to associate a certain feeling on 'Mondays'; mostly a feeling of dread or a certain feeling on 'Saturdays'; usually exciting and a certain feeling on 'Sundays'; the day of 'chilling'. Every day is your creation, every day can be magical and amazing if you decide it to be! Time is precious!

Every moment is an opportunity to be grateful, to feel love, and to be happy. It's all about your perspective. Happiness comes from WITHIN, and when you have happiness within, it doesn't matter what's going on outside of you, you can choose to stay in a happy place! As we all know, life isn't easy, sometimes people annoy us, and things don't go our way. Sometimes we feel unhappy or stressed. You CAN take back your power and still live during these times, it's all inside of you! Happiness is within, things happening outside of you can only affect you if you accept them and let them in. Just like a boat can only sink if the water gets in. Float on that water baby! You got this!

HAVE AN ATTITUDE OF GRATITUDE

Look for something to be grateful for to change how you feel. See the good in every situation. The simple things, the things we take most for granted are life's biggest treasures. You are alive, your heart is beating, you are breathing, you can read this book, you have shelter, and you have food and clean water . . .

If there are things in your life that you don't like, it is so important to change your perspective. Not only will changing your perspective make you feel better NOW, but it will also allow you to change whatever you don't like. You are moving from a negative place to a positive place, and it's when we live in a positive state, that we truly enjoy life, succeed and find happiness! For example, if you have a job that makes you unhappy, first of all you CAN leave, but if for whatever reason you can't at the moment, while you are manifesting your dream job or a better job, you CAN find something to be grateful for. And being grateful now is what allows your dreams to come into reality, so being grateful for your current job will help you get a new job. Complaining about your job will only make you stay there longer! If that job was taken away from you, and then given back to you, t you would appreciate it. So appreciate what you have NOW. Even if it's something simple such as, you like the colour of your pen you are using, you get on well with your colleague, you get to meet interesting people every day. THERE IS ALWAYS SOMETHING TO BE GRATEFUL FOR. Take a moment right now to be thankful for what you have.

> **MAGICAL ACTION**—*Write a list of 20 things you are grateful for every day, do it right now!*

YOU GET WHAT YOU FOCUS ON

If you want to feel good, you have to focus on what makes you feel good!

Focus on what you have and not what you don't have.

Focus on what's working in your life rather than what's not!

Celebrate your wins!

You have a choice of what to focus on; focusing on the bad just gives it more energy and makes it worse, focusing on the good gives the good more energy and therefore you experience more good! You can choose to see the good in every situation in life. Even the dark times in life can be seen as good because they teach us lessons that allow us to grow. They show us something that needs to change, we can then take action on that and therefore create a better reality for ourselves.

It's so easy for us to complain, blame others, look at what we don't have, allow ourselves to be down about the things outside of us that we feel we can't control. No, we cannot control what happens outside of us, but we CAN control how we feel. We can control what we choose to give our attention to. Our attention is our power, when you give something attention it becomes real, it becomes your experience, so the more attention you give to something the more you experience it. Giving your attention to something is asking for more of that thing. When you know this, you can consciously choose to give your attention to the things you actually would like more of, rather than giving attention to what brings you down therefore attracting more things that bring you down, and make you feel stuck! You are never stuck, you can always switch your focus! We can control how we feel inside, how we perceive, how we react, the actions we choose to take, outside things can only affect you if you let them! You have the power, always!

So instead of looking for things to complain about, things that are lacking in your life, and things that make you feel negative emotions, look for things to be grateful for. Focus on the positives. Don't wish your life away and wait for happiness. **Happiness can be right NOW. It's all about your perspective.** Do the things that bring you joy! Feeling good is the key to living in the moment and truly enjoying your life. Do more of what makes you feel good! When you are feeling down, think of how you would rather feel, and then do something that makes you feel that way! Think of what you want to experience, give *that* your attention and energy! Remember, you always have a choice, it's all about your FOCUS.

LIVE YOUR DREAM LIFE NOW

The reason why you want what you want, is not necessarily for that thing, but for the FEELING you will feel when you have it! It can feel like time is just ticking and you are just waiting for that "one day" when you can be happy, when you have your dream partner or house or whatever it is that you desire. Whether you have achieved your dreams or not, today is still your life! It's a precious day that you can't get back! So, find a way to enjoy it, live your dreams today! Instead of waiting for them to come. If you are not happy with where you are now then what makes you think you will be happy with more? Being grateful for what you have now makes you FEEL GOOD! Rather than taking what you have now for granted, appreciate it! One day this day will be just a memory, you will have your dreams but, remember, the journey is the best part. The journey is your life. The people around you won't always be here either, love and appreciate them while you can! Don't get so caught up in chasing happiness that you miss the happiness that can be experienced right now!

Think about each goal you have, think about your dream partner, your dream career, etc. How will you feel when you have those? Write down all of the feelings that you want to feel, that you think reaching your goals will bring to you. Realise, that you CAN feel them now! It may occur by doing different things but it will still bring the feeling! The feeling is what we all crave! The feeling of love, the feeling of excitement, the feeling of joy . . . Find ways to experience those emotions in your everyday, what things could you do every day to bring those feelings? Imagine you were already living the life you desire, do what you would do! Feel how you would feel! Become like a child and use your imagination! Then be in this moment and look at it from a new perspective, a perspective of gratitude.

The very fact that you are breathing right now is a miracle, because someone just took their last breath, just wishing they had more time on this planet. YOU ARE HERE NOW. You are alive NOW. This is the ONLY MOMENT, the past and future are only alive in the mind, they don't exist. Don't let the past hurt you anymore, don't let the future worry you. Choose to be FULLY ALIVE, and live NOW. Thank the past for all of the lessons, for making you who you are today. Forgive yourself and others for past situations. Let your heart be light. Life isn't supposed to be easy, we are here to learn and to grow and if we don't experience the "lows" how can we grow and experience the "highs". It is our perception of situations and labelling them "bad" that make them that way. Next time something happens, try to take yourself out of the situation and see what can be learned, how you can put goodness into that moment. React to situations differently, choosing LOVE over fear. All negative emotions come from a place of fear, the only way they can be transformed is with LOVE. Choose love in every situation and experience here on Earth. Love is the most powerful source in the Universe.

It isn't an emotion, it is who we are! Before everything on this planet got to us, we were born as pure LOVE. A beautiful creation. That is what you are! Love is the greatest feeling and it can be experienced in every moment to live your greatest life, the greatest gift to others and to the planet.

LOVE COMES FROM THE HEART, FEAR COMES FROM THE MIND.

Choose to live from your heart!

LIVING FROM THE HEART

- GRATITUDE
- KINDNESS
- COMPASSION
- EXCITEMENT
- PASSION
- JOY/ HAPPINESS
- UNDERSTANDING
- CONNECTION
- APPRECIATION
- POSITIVITY
- PEACE

BASICALLY ALL OF THE THINGS THAT FEEL GOOD, COME FROM THE HEART!

The present moment is the key to truly living. A lot of people (myself included) have spent time never fully here, in my mind I was reliving a past memory or I was thinking about a future event. I was playing a situation in my mind, making myself worried or anxious and affecting how I was living in that moment. I did this not realising that by doing it, and living in my mind, I was causing myself to miss the very moment I was currently living; missing the joy that can be experienced right now and the moment I can never live again. The most important thing in life is to enjoy the NOW. Live in the present, appreciate the present.

> **MAGICAL ACTION**—*Practise meditation to stop overthinking, bring yourself back to the present by feeling the temperature, focusing energy to a part of your body, focusing on your breath. Realise you are not your thoughts, observe them instead of being attached to them and they will no longer have power over you!*

TAKE CHANCES, GET OUT OF YOUR COMFORT ZONE

Your comfort zone stops you from truly living, it stops you from growing! We were made to grow, to evolve, to experience. Start taking risks, take opportunities, go on more adventures. Do things that scare you that you really want to do but you stop yourself from doing, such as silly things like singing out loud in the street. I now do this all the time and it feels damn good!Life was made to live! If you wait until you are ready for opportunities, you will never be ready and you will never do it! That opportunity may never come again. So do it now! Jump first and you can figure it out later! Always say "yes" to opportunities that feel good and would help you grow and become better! Challenge yourself! You will never get this moment again. Not taking chances can lead to regret and can never be taken back! If something feels right, don't take a second thought, just DO IT!

Your comfort zone can turn into your prison. If we are comfortable, we get lazy and start to procrastinate. We live the same life over and over again if we don't make the decision to get out of our comfort zone and make changes! **TIME IS ALL WE HAVE**, it must be used wisely. Some people tiptoe through life, hoping to make it safely to death. Truth is, none of us are making it out alive, and so what is the point in being comfortable? PUSH YOURSELF to grow. There are no limits, keep learning new things, conquering fears, taking risks. Grow and grow, be better and better.

This is something that I wrote on my wall to look at every day to remind me to LIVE NOW.

TODAY IS THE BEST DAY EVER
YOU ARE STILL ALIVE!
YOUR BODY IS WORKING NATURALLY
YOU ARE BREATHING
YOUR HEART IS BEATING
BE GRATEFUL FOR EVERYTHING
SEE LOVE AND GIVE LOVE TO EVERYTHING
APPRECIATE THE SMALL THINGS
BE SILLY, HAVE FUN!
REMEMBER THE WORLD WOULD RUN WITHOUT YOU
DON'T TAKE LIFE OR YOURSELF TOO SERIOUSLY
YOU GET WHAT YOU GIVE ATTENTION TO AND
YOU HAVE A CHOICE!

BE GREAT!
ENJOY LIFE!
THIS IS THE ONLY MOMENT YOU HAVE!
LIVE NOW.

The things that make me feel truly ALIVE, my inspirations for life and remembering who I am

- The moon
- The forest
- The stars
- The sky
- Trees
- Mother Nature as a whole
- Music, singing and performing
- Creating/Expression
- Soul connection with people and animals
- Deep Conversation
- Travelling/ adventures
- Helping others
- The feeling after exercise
- The greats that remind me of who I am (Jimi Hendrix, MJ, Prince, etc.)
- Rainstorms
- Sunshine
- Alice in Wonderland
- Native Americans

- Shamans
- Crystals
- Magical other worldly beings (obv), unicorns, aliens, fairies, etc.
- Wolves
- Street art/ graffiti
- Poetry
- NYC and Los Angeles
- 1990's
- Disco/70s/soul music
- Dancehall music and dance
- Flowers, especially daisies and sunflowers

And soooo much more!

WHAT INSPIRES YOU AND MAKES YOU FEEL TRULY ALIVE?

LOVE YOURSELF FIRST

SELF-LOVE IS NOT SELFISH, IT IS ESSENTIAL

We are all seeking love. Love is the greatest feeling in the world, it is the feeling of truly being alive. Realising that love comes from within is the greatest revelation. You are only ever going to be you, so LOVE YOURSELF. Don't resist who you are meant to be, you are greatness, you are incredible. You are the only you there will ever be and that is so fucking special! Enjoy being YOU! I believe self-love is the healing of the world. If everyone on this planet loved themselves truly, the world would be a beautiful place to live. For when you love yourself, you can live your best life, you can truly love and give to others, and you can enjoy your time here on Earth! You loving yourself before loving others is not selfish. Often we hear "Oh they love themselves" as a negative statement, it is associated with vanity, narcissism and selfishness. We are told it is selfish to love yourself, we must always put others first, others are worth more than us, others needs must be met before our own . . .

This is the opposite of self-love! Self-love is making sure you are full before you give to others. How can you give love if you first don't have it to give? You cannot give what you don't have.

I used to be such a "people pleaser", always putting others' needs before my own, and completely draining myself. I didn't know who I was anymore because I was too busy depending on others and trying to make others approve of me. I just wanted to be a good person and I spent so much time trying to prove it to receive love and validation from others.

Now, I truly realise that I need to love myself first. *Then* I can give to others, I can be my best for others. There is no point in me trying to help others unless I've helped myself, I can't give what I don't have and I can't then do my best for them, which doesn't benefit them, or me.

Learn to say no, set boundaries, protect your energy! It's not wrong to say no to someone, it is self-care, self-respect! It's important to take care of yourself first, and the people that truly love you will understand that. If something doesn't feel right, then don't do it. Look after yourself.

It took me a long time to learn that it was okay to say no. I wanted to help others but felt so guilty saying no, I never wanted to let anyone down because I knew what it felt like. As a child, whenever I had plans with someone, I would get so excited and then they would let me down last minute and I would feel crushed! So I never cancelled any plans, I never said no to anyone asking me to do something with them or for them. I didn't want them to feel what I felt. But in doing this I was putting myself in uncomfortable situations, like going out and drinking when I really didn't want to. This was me just looking for acceptance. Or, sleeping with guys because I felt like I had to, I felt like I couldn't say no. I felt awkward for saying no to people, even when I was compromising myself. Saying no is taking back your power. Saying no is also saying "I'm important and I love and respect myself enough to only do what feels right to me." Like I said, that is the only way we can give our best to others, if we truly want to be there! If we say yes to someone and don't really want to do it, we can't give our best energy and the other person wouldn't benefit, saying no when it feels right is best for everyone!

If you don't love yourself first, you can become attached to others, you can have expectations of others. You will rely on others to give you love, and even if they do, it won't fill that space that can only be filled by loving yourself. When you are filled, you love yourself, only then can you truly give unconditionally to others. Others will benefit more from you. Otherwise you will be drained, because you are giving too much and running yourself empty. What use is that in life?

Fill yourself up first, make sure your cup is overflowing and then you will be able to give to others, but not lose anything within you.

"CLOSE YOUR EYES AND IMAGINE THE BEST VERSION OF YOU POSSIBLE, THAT IS WHO YOU TRULY ARE, LET GO OF ANY PART OF YOU THAT DOESN'T BELIEVE THAT".—C. Assad

To be the best version of yourself, to give the best to others, to truly make a difference in the world, you must first LOVE YOURSELF.

Self-love is the greatest discovery I made on my journey. I always saw me loving myself as me thinking I'm better than others, which of course I don't think, so I never put any importance on self-love. I was seeking outside of myself for love, I was seeking approval, especially from men. I thought if a man loved me that would complete me and I would be worthy. But when I didn't love myself, if a man I liked was speaking to someone else, even liked someone's picture online, thought another girl was pretty or didn't give me the full attention I craved, I would feel insecure and jealous. I would just want someone to want me and be with me so that I felt worthy. I wanted someone who depended on me for love, so that they would never leave me and I felt loved always. Whereas now that I LOVE MYSELF, I am very happily 'single' and will not settle for anything less than someone magical, someone who also loves themselves—that is the only way they could truly love me. Because I LOVE MYSELF, I know my worth, I know I only want to be with someone who comes from a place of unconditional love and not lust for my physical appearance, or a need to receive love from me because they don't have it within. An equal exchange of two souls who love themselves and want to share that with each other is what I want.

Loving myself allows me to know when someone truly loves me and truly has the best intentions for me. I have higher standards, and that's a very good thing, I only choose to live my best life, with beautiful people around me. People that give to each other because they are full. When I meet the right man for me, we will both love ourselves and be happy alone, so then we won't expect anything of each other, we will CHOOSE to be with each other, instead of 'NEEDING' to be with each other. Needing someone is not a good or romantic thing. You must be complete while alone first! Saying you need someone is saying you are incomplete without this person, which you are not! You are a whole, beautiful incredible person alone!

> "Find yourself first,
> What you love,
> What turns you on
> And how to be at peace;
> Then never settle for anyone
> Who doesn't compliment you,
> And give you even more of
> What you already have."—Mark Anthony

You know when someone loves themselves truly. You can see and feel it! When you love yourself truly, your presence will light up the room. People will want to be around you because you automatically radiate love and beautiful energy.

We are here to live our own lives. You should be able to be with someone but also live your own life. Your number one love should be yourself. Even if you have children, if you don't love yourself you won't be able to give to your children as much as you could if you were first full. Same with your partner, friends, family, THE WORLD.

Loving yourself, having self-confidence and self-worth makes you INDESTRUCTIBLE.

How to Love Yourself

LEARN TO LOVE BEING ALONE

Spending time by yourself is so essential for self-love. I used to hate being alone, it would make me feel like no one wanted to spend time with me, so it made my self-worth so low. But now I am literally alone most of the time, I am my own best friend! I LOVE spending time alone. Time to recharge, check in with myself and give myself some love! Alone time doesn't have to feel lonely, you are all you need! Start enjoying time by yourself. It's your charging time so you can give to others, so you can truly enjoy others' company, because you enjoy your own. When you enjoy your own company you will know true friendship and will choose to spend time with others, just like in relationships, once you love yourself and have been alone, you accept only the best in other connections. Ones that add value and don't just drain your energy! Don't be afraid to be alone!

It's quite possible that you may be the only person that believes in your dreams. You may not fit in, you may have a different mindset than others and feel like you are playing small to make others feel comfortable. It's time to stop living to please others. Learn to say no. You must look after yourself first. Honor yourself. **Don't be afraid to let go of negative relationships, or situations that hold you back.**

Only by spending time alone can you get to know yourself, can you truly love yourself and find your true life path. It's blocking out the noise of everyone else's opinions and focusing on your own inner voice. To follow your dreams, you have to stop caring about what other people think. **You're not going to be here one day, so live for YOU.**

No, it's not easy to be alone, but it is worth it. Once you spend time alone, getting to know, love, heal and improve yourself, you can be the best version of yourself. Therefore, achieving your dreams, and finding your 'tribe', which has the same vision as you, brings a TRUE connection and you can elevate and encourage each other.

BELIEVE IN YOURSELF

THE most important factor in achieving your goals and living your best life is believing in yourself. **Knowing that there is and will only ever be one you. Your life is up to you and no one else.** No one can tell you what you really want, only you know that. No one else can tell you how to live your life, you have a choice. Accept what others choose for your reality, or create your own. **You must be confident within yourself and have no doubt that you will achieve your goals.** If we love ourselves and believe in ourselves, then nothing anyone says will stop us. You do not have to live the life your parents want for you, or society says you should, or your teachers taught you, YOU CHOOSE YOUR LIFE.

Encourage yourself, uplift yourself, and motivate yourself. **The person we speak to the most is ourselves so make sure you are saying kind things.** Don't be hard on yourself, **CELEBRATE WHO YOU ARE.** Realise that a lot of the things you tell yourself and believe about yourself have come from someone else's lack of love for themselves. When someone isn't happy within themselves, they will try to bring you down to make themselves feel better. Which is why people may have told you that you're not good enough, you're not worthy, and you're not beautiful or any other bullshit like that! YOU ARE INCREDIBLE! It's time to start believing it!

MAGICAL ACTION—*Write a list of all the things you believe about yourself, things you tell yourself every day. Rip up the bad ones and write new, positive ones! Write all of the things you love about yourself. Even if it's little at the moment, the more positive you are about yourself, the more the things you love will grow! Write what you want to be, and believe you are that! Because you are!*

It's time to believe in yourself. Everything you wish you could be, you already are. It's waiting there inside of you to be awakened again. Remember what I said in the beginning about you being born as a miracle; you are a beautiful, incredible, and special LIFE! No one else can determine who you are, that is your choice. You choose who you want to be, you choose what to believe. So write a positive list of things you want to be, and write "I AM' in front of them, i.e. "I AM BEAUTIFUL", "I AM SUCCESSFUL", and "I AM ENOUGH"

Put this list somewhere you can see it every day and read it out loud. Say them with feeling. Feel what it is to be what you wrote down! Keep doing this every day until you believe it. Celebrate all of your little wins, realise all you've been through and you are still here, you're doing so great! All of the little good things that you do, celebrate them, recognise them as progress. Focus on all of your positive aspects instead of the negative. Instead of looking in the mirror and finding flaws, look for things you like. Speak about the things you don't like, as though you actually love them. Be thankful for all that you are and all that you have. Someone else may be wishing for what you have. Focus on your positive traits, all of the nice things you do; your gifts. Focus on this and nothing else, until you love every part of yourself. Then, nothing can stop you.

EXPRESS YOURSELF

Throughout my childhood, I went through different phases of who I was. I was in different groups or "cliques" which were defined by labels. So the end of primary school/beginning of high school I was an "alternative kid" ,"goth" ,"emo" ,"mosher" to name a few of the labels to define the style. I listened to Green Day, My Chemical Romance, Fall Out Boy, etc. I went to a club called 'Cathouse', hung out in Central Station, longed to be "myspace famous" and in school there was a certain area where the "alternative kids" hung out. Then I was an "indie kid" I bought NME magazines every month, I dressed like the lead singer of my favourite band at the time, Kyle Falconer from The View, I shopped mostly in Topshop, wore Fred Perry shirts, I went to gigs all the time. Then, in the hip-hop phase, I started my own dance crew-inspired by the Step Up movies, I hung around with certain people in certain places, I wore Baby Phat, Apple Bottoms, Billionaire Boys Club, etc.

The point of me talking about this is, we don't have to be defined by a label and we don't have to be put into a box. I think the phase I felt most free was my "alternative kid" phase, I felt like I was rebelling, we were the "weirdos" and I loved it. However, I did hide my love for Britney Spears and Pussycat Dolls and listened to them secretly so I wouldn't seem "uncool".

In my late teens and early twenties I longed for designer clothes. Anything that was cool, created or worn by a celebrity that I liked. Whatever was "on trend", in magazines and that everyone wanted, I wanted. So I'd spend a majority of my wages on a designer pair of trainers or bag or whatever, to give myself a sense of worth. A sense of "being someone" because I had these things. I made myself broke to look rich. It all seems so silly to me now. If designer clothes are your thing, no disrespect to you, keep doing you! But for me, I know I wanted designer clothes because we are made to believe that they make us more important. It is truly looking for a sense of self-worth from something because of the name that's on it. It could be the same piece of clothing, but those letters, that word written on it, makes the price much higher. They advertise that you are a desired, successful individual because you have that thing. It's like you are worth more as a human being because your possessions are worth more, which is complete bullshit. Looking for happiness in possessions, brands, and labels will always be a disappointment. When one trend is done, they bring out a new trend, then you suddenly feel like you need that new thing, it's never ending!

People shouldn't be judged, you shouldn't have to be defined by a certain label, and only listen to certain music, wear certain clothes, follow what celebrities do and wear, etc. JUST BE YOU! Be free and like whatever the heck you want to like.

I really feel uncomfortable being defined by labels, I'm just me! I'm a mix of everything I used to be and more; I love so many different types of music, I wear whatever the heck I want to wear, whatever makes me feel good and feel like me.

Embrace ALL sides of you and set them all free!

I believe everyone should be free to be who they truly are. Who **THEY choose to be**. Not who they are told to be by society, magazines, trends, labels. We should be encouraged and empowered to express who we truly are to the world, without fear of judgement, without separation.

UNITED IN OUR UNIQUENESS.

Imagine how *beautiful, colourful and free* the world would feel if we all just allowed ourselves to be who we truly want to be, wear what makes us **FEEL GOOD**. Our light shines so bright when we feel good, and that then spreads to everyone we meet! **Raising the vibration of the world, through our self-love.**

Style, to me, is something that expresses the spirit within you to the world. Because we only see the physical, the clothes we wear and how we choose to decorate our bodies, it is the expression of who we are within.

Through loving and being true to yourself, shining your light and your true magic within, you inspire others to do the same, and guide them to their own light. Therefore living our greatest lives, as our truest selves, raising the vibration on Earth (love is the highest frequency), **LOVE IS HEALING.**

This is my vision for my clothing creations **11.11 EARTH**. A positive, uplifting, inspiring, magical, empowering **MOVEMENT** of love and peace, through expression of **TRUE SELF.** I call it a **MOVEMENT** and not a 'clothing line' as the intention is to spread LOVE and beautiful energy, peace and unity. To create a free and safe space to be who you truly are and feel accepted, loved and a part of something beautiful. To unite, we have to love ourselves and love each other by being true to ourselves.

That's what I believe about our time on this planet, we are all here together, we are one, I believe in unity and harmony. Being true to who you are and feeling free to express yourself is so important. I believe everyone should be free to be who they choose to be, to express themselves from their soul, without fear of what others think, or not fitting in, or being "on trend". Style is a beautiful form of art to me. I have so much fun everyday expressing myself with my appearance. I feel like I am showing who I am to the world, showing them who they are by me showing who I am. Your appearance doesn't matter, it's not who you are, it's who you are within that matters. Appearance is just an extension of yourself. Wear what makes YOU happy! You are a masterpiece. Don't just save your favourite clothes, clothes that make you feel good, for special occasions, feel good every day! Every day on Earth is a special occasion!

DO WHAT MAKES YOU HAPPY

This is key to loving yourself. It feels good when you do what you love! That is being true to yourself. Give yourself time every day to do something that you truly love. Whether that's drawing, singing, swimming, D.I.Y, whatever it is, just do it! Do the things that make you feel free! Do the things that bring you joy, everyone has something that makes them feel so happy! For me it is singing, performing and creating! That is when I feel truly alive and in the moment, it comes from my soul. Nothing else matters when I'm doing what I love, I am fully present and enjoying every moment! Whatever makes you feel like that, make sure you do that as often as possible! You have your hobbies and loves for a reason. They are unique to you, even though other people do those things, they don't do them like you. Embrace your natural gifts.

MAGICAL ACTION—*Write two lists, one of the things you do every day and then next to that write a list of the things you love, the things that make you feel happy. Compare the two. How often do you do what you love? Adjust the lists accordingly. Do more of what you love every day to enjoy your life, and give yourself the love you deserve.*

YOUR VIBE ATTRACTS YOUR TRIBE

FRIENDSHIPS AND RELATIONSHIPS

Our time on Earth is so precious. It is so important who you choose to surround yourself with in your time here. YOU HAVE A CHOICE! You become like the people you surround yourself with.

What kind of person do you want to be?

How do you want to feel?

What do you want to do with your life?

Are you surrounding yourself with people that reflect this?

Think about the person you want to be. The greatest version of yourself, which is who you truly are. You should be surrounding yourself with people who bring out that version of you, people who truly SUPPORT, LOVE and ELEVATE you! People who you can be COMPLETELY yourself around!

I spent so much time surrounding myself with people I couldn't be myself around. I moulded myself to try and fit in with them and be 'accepted'. I was scared to be alone and to have no friends, so I would be with people who, when I see from my perspective now, weren't really my true friends. It's not selfish to let go of people who don't serve your highest good and bring out the best in you. It IS selfish to stay friends with them because not only do you deserve to be around people you truly resonate with, THEY DO TOO! If you cannot truly be your best self, and give your best to someone, then it is unfair to stay in that person's life just because you feel too uncomfortable to let go. You would be hurting that person more by being untrue to yourself.

WE ALL DESERVE TO BE SURROUNDED BY OUR TRUE SOUL TRIBE!

It is the greatest feeling to be in a friendship where you can truly be yourself. At your worst and your best, that person will still be your friend through it all. It goes back to self-love, when we love ourselves we trust in our friendships more. We cannot talk to our friends and we still know and they still know how much they mean to us and that we are still there. There is no neediness or requirement to speak every single day and take on your friends' problems and be expected of. Friends are there to support and love each other, but we also have our own lives and are on our own journeys and our true friends understand and love that!

Your friends should be encouraging you, supporting you. Your friends should be your biggest fans, supporting all of your dreams! I have had friends in my life that were great friends when I was down, but when I was at my best they didn't like it! Stay away from those types of friends! True friends should love your through the downs and the ups, they should be overjoyed to see you being great! True friends inspire and motivate each other! My friends and I now are like each other's "accountability partners", we check in with each other and make sure we are doing things every day that help us grow and feel good and be our best selves! Friendships are teamwork! No competing, or comparing! If you have a friend that constantly wants to have better things than you, knows better than you or had what you have before you did, that's not a real friend! Someone who doesn't love themselves can't be a real friend to others because they can't truly support their friends' success because they don't follow their own dreams! This can bring you down if you have friends that make you feel guilty or unworthy of your dreams. Surround yourself with people who are also following their dreams and being true to themselves, that's when you get a true friendship! There needs to be a resonance! Similar interests, goals, mindsets, etc. That's how you become a true team, you relate to each other! They bring out the best version of you, the true you!

I love that the friends I now have in my life have pure intentions and truly support and love me, because they also love themselves and are on their own true path. I met these friends when I truly loved and knew myself. I spent a lot of time alone just longing for my soul tribe to appear, but I knew they would only come when I was truly ME. I needed that time alone to find myself first. I still do love time alone and am alone most of the time, I am my own best friend! Get to know and love yourself FIRST and then you will truly know who you want to surround yourself with and won't accept anything less!

It's the same with relationships. Because I didn't love myself, I thought I needed to be with a man, I craved attention and acceptance from men. Boys never liked me in school and I felt so shit about myself, I would change myself to make the boy I liked, like me back, and of course they never did! So my self-worth felt so low and that continued and was the reason why I was in long relationships in my late teens and early twenties. When my relationship with someone I was with for two and a half years ended, I was broken. I thought we were going to get married, live happily ever after, all of that! Little did I know, I didn't even know who I was then. After him, I decided I didn't want to miss out on what 'every other' 20 odd year old gets to do with their life. Partying, drinking, dating, etc. I'd never enjoyed clubs or drinking, I just did it to fit in, but I felt like I would have regretted it if I didn't at least try it. So for around 8 months I worked in a night-club, got drunk, kissed guys, dated some people and genuinely had fun doing it. It felt good to feel like I was a part of something. I then went on a working holiday to work in clubs and again 'do what everyone else was doing'. Deep down, I was craving connection, deep conversations and meaning. All I found was drinking, drugs, sex, and a general lack of meaning. I was treated as a sexual object, I slept with a few boys, got drunk pretty much every night, and ate food that was bad for me. It quickly got old. No disrespect if you enjoy doing these things, we are all on our own journeys. But my point is, I ALWAYS knew it wasn't for me, but I went against who I was to try and fit in. But I am so thankful for the experience because every part of my journey has made me who I am now and I've learned from every experience.

After my partying stage, I met a guy from New York whom I quickly fell hard for; more than I ever have for anyone. He was everything I imagined my perfect man to be in many ways. It felt too good to be true. I was insanely attracted to him and he was very mysterious and intriguing. I was entranced. He wasn't like anyone I'd ever met. I just wanted to know him and love him. I thought he was too good for me. So I wasn't myself around him. I tried to be 'cool' to make him love me. To not seem too interested in him, to keep my feelings inside, to act like I wasn't bothered. I didn't even really speak that much because I was scared to say something he wouldn't like and he wouldn't like me anymore. I was treading on eggshells because I was scared to lose him. I was so incredibly hypnotised by him, and at this point in my life, I didn't know my worth. I thought I knew who I was, I thought I loved myself but I really didn't. I never ever told him how I felt about him, I was too scared he would think I was weird and reject me—just like I was used to during my childhood. So I played it cool, which in fact was really just not being myself. When he stopped talking to me when I came back from NYC, I was truly broken. I spent months and months in a very dark, deep depression. He was literally all I thought of. I spent my time listening to songs that reminded me of him, I wrote deep poetry about him and how I felt. I was in a hole, a shadow of myself. It must have been scary for my family and friends because I was in a very bad place. I just wanted to be with him, that's all I cared about. So because I wasn't, I just didn't even want to be on the planet anymore, every day was a drag. It was very painful.

But it was the best thing that ever happened to me, that he rejected me, at that time I just wanted to be with him so badly, but if I did get what I wanted I would be less of myself than I even was before because he would have become my life and I wouldn't be who I am today. I went to such a dark place because of the rejection that it forced me to go within myself to find who I truly was and since then, I have been on the most incredible, beautiful journey of evolving and living a life from my soul. I was living my true purpose, knowing why I'm on the planet. All while still healing from loving him, it didn't go away and being honest, it is still there, but in a different way. I know he is not meant for me, at this time anyway. However, I have a lot of gratitude and love for him and always will.

I now truly know who I am, and I am in the best relationship I have ever been in, with MYSELF. Learning every single day to love myself and heal from all of the past mindsets and habits that don't serve me, I can't be rejected anymore. The only person that can reject me is me and I FUCKING LOVE MYSELF! So other people rejecting me doesn't affect me anymore, I know it has nothing to do with me, I don't take it personally. And now I know what I truly want when I'm going to be with a man. I know who would be meant for me, because I KNOW ME! I wouldn't settle for anything less, because I'm happy alone! I could only be with someone who added to what I already have, because being with myself is incredible. I just no longer see the point in being with someone, just to be with someone, because I have all the love I need within me. My cup of love has to be full and overflowing, and so does his. So we can then share with each other but not lose anything within ourselves. We should not depend on each other for happiness or love because we have it alone. I feel like society makes needing someone look romantic and loving, but for me I feel like you shouldn't *need* someone else, they should just be an addition to who you already are. CHOOSING someone instead of needing someone, you don't need to be with them because you are happy alone, but you CHOOSE to be with them. Is much more powerful and truly loving, rather than needing, someone.

Needing someone implies you are incomplete without that person, when you are a complete person on your own! You should have everything you need within YOU. Then you can truly give to and unconditionally love your partner, and if for whatever reason one day you grow apart, you won't be attached to them and try to make them stay with you. Their happiness will be all that matters to you. When you truly, truly, unconditionally love someone, you just want them to be happy! Whether that's with you or not, it doesn't matter! Like I said, we are all on our own paths and we meet people for a reason, a season or a lifetime. Some people are temporary in our lives and are only meant for that time and who we are at that time, and that's okay! We are here to grow and change, and sometimes people change in different directions. We should be able to happily accept that and see it as normal and keep carrying on with our journeys!

So, the conclusion of "your vibe attracts your tribe" is literally that. When you are being truly yourself, you attract your tribe! Your true friends, your true love! Only when you are being your true self can you attract who is meant to join you on your life journey! I talk more about this in the chapter "Go Your Own Way".

MAGICAL ACTION—*Make a list of all of the qualities you would like your friends to have, how you want to feel around your friends, etc. and the same for a relationship. Then don't settle for anything less!*

RELEASE YOUR INNER CHILD

Think back to when you were a child. You truly knew who you were, you lived in the moment, you created, you had fun, and you believed in MAGIC; you saw the Earth through magical eyes. You were a true Unicorn. You didn't think about the past or future, you didn't worry about what others thought of you or what your ex was doing, etc. You were FREE! Life was a huge adventure. You just wanted to play and enjoy life. You were purely love!

Every day was different, there was a new amazing adventure to have! You were discovering every single day and you were playing constantly!

Then the adults started feeding our mind, telling us what was right and wrong, how to live, who to be and we started to fear. Eventually you became a product of everyone else beliefs, whether it was your parents, schools, or friends. Whether you realise it or not, everything you are now is a mixture of everything you have been taught and accepted as truth. It's no one's fault, your parents did the best they could, and they taught you what they know!

Look around you every day, how many adults do you see that are happy like children? And when you do see that, how rare is it? People look crazy when they are adults acting like children. It's seen as normal to be a miserable adult, to have responsibilities, to stop being "childish", and to "grow up". Pay your bills, work, etc. The adults have forgotten who they truly are! I don't know about you but I would much rather be "childish" or "crazy" than "grown up" if grown up means being boring and miserable.

As a child we did what we loved, we had love within us! And we expressed that love freely! Now as adult you chase love outside of yourself, it's became about what loves you, gaining peoples approval, buying the latest products, getting more customers, worrying about how you look etc. Children don't think about any of this!

For so long I was such an "anti-children" person, like keep your kids away from me! Kids irritated me so much because they were so hyper and happy. Now, I realise why adults get annoyed with kids, because kids are happy and the adults are miserable! When you're a child all you want to do is be grown up, but when you're an adult you just wish you could go back to being a kid again! Well, you still can.

The key to being who you truly are in life and living your best life, is to KEEP YOUR INNER CHILD ALIVE.

Connect with that place within you, remember who you were as a child. Not what might have happened to you or any bad memories, but your pure loving energy, your desire to explore, to create, to give love and just ENJOY LIFE!

Look at life through the eyes of a child, feel the wonder and the magic of discovering new things every day, meeting new people, exploring the planet and all of the beauty it has to offer. Every day of your life can be a new adventure! You don't have to do the same things every single day, have FUN!

When "adult" life gets to be too much for me, I remember myself as a child. I connect with her, I'll listen to the music I listened to as a child, watch my favourite childhood movies and I feel full of joy! I truly live for little Leah Luna Lightwarrior, she knew who she was and who she wanted to be. Now I live her dreams every day, I want her to be proud of who she has become. Our inner child is our truth, they are counting on us to live the life they wanted to live! Don't let them down! Give love to your inner child.

Never forget who you were as a child; the dreams you had, your imagination, your fun and creativity! Your "I don't give a shit about what people think of me" attitude! Your focus is on the moment and the MAGIC of life!

SET YOUR CREATIVITY FREE

Your creativity is your magic. You don't have to be a professional artist to be creative. You don't have to be good at it. There is no good and bad creativity. You are a natural born artist of life. Your life is your creation. There is no good or bad, there is only expressing yourself. Expressing yourself is a beautiful thing. EVERYONE is creative, it is a natural part of being human, and when you are creating you are fully in the moment. For me when I create, whether it's singing, painting jackets, writing poetry, etc., I feel the most alive. I appreciate the moment, I am fully immersed in what I am doing. I feel FREE! Then I also have achieved something at the end of it because I've created something that wasn't there before. When you create, it is from a place of NO MIND. All your worries and thinking about the past and future disappear. The greatest artists, musicians and creative people in the world all create from a place of no mind. When you are in a place of no mind, you are connected to the power of who you are, the power of the Universe, the higher power— whatever that means for you.

DO THE THINGS THAT MAKE YOU FEEL ALIVE

Whatever that is for you! Those times when you feel truly full of joy, whether it is as simple as singing in the shower, hanging out with your best friend, going for a relaxing walk, DO MORE OF THOSE THINGS!

Make your everyday tasks FUN! Find ways to enjoy the things that seem mundane or boring. If I'm cleaning I will play some Michael Jackson or Prince or another artist or music that makes me feel good, I blast it around the house or listen in my ear phones and dance while I clean! And think about how grateful I am to have a warm home to live in. When I'm doing my grocery shopping I will take my earphones and listen to my favourite music and dance and sing down the aisles! (This may not be easy for you at this point but trust me it will come!) Everyday of your life is to be enjoyed, you never know when it's your last. So stop taking life so seriously, like we are told adults should and let your inner child come alive and HAVE FUN!

EXPLORE AND ADVENTURE

There is so much to be experienced in life, you don't have to do the same things every day! Each day can be different, each day can be a new adventure. Discover new things, research things that interest you, learn more! It's exciting when you learn new things you didn't know before, just like when a child learns new things! We are in a constant state of learning in life and it's exciting! Explore new places, you don't have to necessarily travel the world to do this, visit local places, find places you've never been before. Do something spontaneous and go on a trip! Do random exciting things! When I was a kid I remember my mum used to do a "mystery tour" and we would just get in the car with no destination and just pick each direction she drove, then end up in a new place. It was exciting! Do things like this to keep life fun and fresh! We have a full planet of beautiful things to discover and enjoy while we are here, make the most of it!

BE SILLY

Have fun! Lots of it! Don't take life so seriously. The world would keep going if you died tomorrow, so live in the now and enjoy your time here. Taking yourself and life seriously takes away the fun! You start to think there's things you can and can't do. Fuck that. Do silly things, act like a child. Laugh more, *play*! Speak in a funny voice, make up new words, and dance like no one is watching! Actually, dance when everyone is watching! Give yourself permission to enjoy yourself without caring what other people think of it! Like I said before, your tribe will join you and start silly dancing WITH you!

STOP "ACTING YOUR AGE"

I always hear people say "Oh I can't do that anymore, I'm too old for that", when considering doing something they'd love to do, something that would make them really happy. Get those limitations out of your head. There is no certain rules for certain ages, you don't have to act or dress a certain way just because you are a certain age. Be you! Age doesn't define who you are, don't stop being you and doing the things you want to do because of your age! It's just a number. You are an ageless soul, you are how you feel! You don't have to "act your age", what is an age supposed to act like? We are all unique, we are all individuals! Is every 40-year-old supposed to act the same? Is every 80-year-old supposed to act the same? NO! Be you! Be free! Don't let your age make you feel limited to what you can do with your life. Life is here to be lived! We are here to experience every age, but don't let it change who you truly are. The best example of this is the badass grandma "Baddie Winkle", she doesn't give a fuck what anyone thinks! She doesn't act like an "89 year old is supposed to act". She does what she wants to do! And she is a magical AF Unicorn!!!

USE YOUR IMAGINATION

Your imagination is your true power! It is how you create your reality! Use your imagination every day to imagine the kind of day you want to have today, imagine your best day ever and feel what it would be like to experience that. Carry that feeling throughout your day and I guarantee you will experience magic! Imagine your perfect life, take yourself to other worlds! Open your mind to the fact that this physical world isn't the only reality! I have personally experienced that it's not! Imagination is the fuel of a child, it brings magic to life and in the simplest things there is magic to be found, use your imagination!

MAGICAL ACTION—*If you have a child in your life, spend the day with them and really see the world the way they see it, allow yourself to let go of your worries and your "adulting" and gain wisdom from a child! Think of how you were as a child, what made you happy, what did you do, how did you see the world? Take action on fulfilling the happiness of your inner child! Never grow up!*

BE, BEFORE YOU DO

Your first purpose is to be a human BEING. Don't get so caught up in the fast pace of society and believing we have to be doing something all the time, especially if you live in the city. Don't do' so much that you forget to live. Some people get so busy being busy that they don't truly live their lives. Yes, we have actions to take in life every day, however it is important that you FEEL GOOD BEFORE YOU TAKE ACTION. Nothing productive and worthwhile is ever done when you are not feeling good. When you feel good you are at your best therefore you can do your best. You can give 100% only if you HAVE 100%! So make sure every day you get yourself into a POSITIVE STATE before you take action! When you are feeling good, you are aligned with your true power. You make better decisions from a place of feeling good! You are seeing life from a higher perspective!

To have a great day, it is essential to have a great morning. How you spend your mornings determine how your day will go. A morning routine is essential to living a great life! At the moment, just assuming like most people, the first thing you probably do in the morning is check your phone, or think about what you've got to do today, or think about what happened yesterday, etc. Starting your day like this is what makes the rest of the day not too great! Think about this. When you check your phone as soon as you open your eyes, let's say you scroll through Facebook or Instagram, and you see something that pisses you off! Or you open your emails and your boss has sent you something that makes you dread your day! Doing this is giving your power away, it's letting other people control how your day goes, because this controls how you feel and how you feel is everything. If you start your day with a morning routine of an hour or so or whatever time you can JUST FOR YOU and feeling good, then when you go on your phone, you are better equipped to handle what you see! When you feel good, things don't bother you as much. When you wake up you are vulnerable, you have been sleeping, so that is the time when you can control what you think and how you feel! Your power is within how you choose to start your day.

You choose to have a great day by choosing to have a great morning! By waking up and deciding "TODAY IS GOING TO BE A GREAT DAY!" What you say, think and do is what you attract. You have to make a conscious decision that your day is going to be amazing! Sure, sleeping in feels great but it sets us up to be lazy and essentially we are missing precious hours of life that you can't get back! Especially if you have big goals, sleeping in is not going to help you achieve those goals! I wake up in the morning and think "Do I still have goals to achieve?" And if the answer is yes, I know I need to get my butt out of bed and make the most of the day! I will sleep in when I have achieved my goals, probably not even then because there is always greater heights to be reached in life. Every day is an opportunity to grow and be better!

Discipline is required for this, it's not going to be easy when you just want to lay in your warm cosy bed, and the mind does everything it can to convince you to just stay in bed. When your alarm goes off you literally have a few seconds to just force yourself to get up! Otherwise your brain will kick in and sweet talk you into just staying in bed a little longer. Decide to have control over your brain and literally jump your body out of bed! To be successful, start with getting up early. The most successful people wake up at 5 a.m., we have limited time on this planet so make the most of your time here. I can hear you saying what I said when I first discovered this "But, I'm not a morning person!"

TRUST ME once you get into a routine of having a great morning you will realise just how precious and important the morning truly is. Wake up a bit earlier than normal to make time for you and making yourself feel good! Think about how easy the rest of your day will be when you've done the hardest thing, which is get yourself out of bed in the morning! That's an achievement itself, its only uphill from there.

Waking up in the morning is a true blessing, you get to have another day of life! Keep this in mind when you wake up in the morning!

Here are some suggestions of a morning routine, this is what I do to start my day. If you work, get up an hour earlier than normal and make time for a morning routine, before you get ready to go out! It will make a huge difference to your day and is worth getting up earlier to do!

MEDITATION: Meditation helps you focus on your breathing, being fully present in the moment (which is all there is, there is only now), being present is fully living, and becoming detached from the mind. Realising you have control of your thoughts, and you are not your mind. You will still have thoughts while meditating, it's only natural! For so long I got annoyed at myself for thinking while meditating, but everyone does it. That's the point. It's not about stopping the thoughts, but being able to observe them and watch them float by like clouds, not giving any attention to them. You are not your thoughts because you are also listening to your thoughts. You are the observer of the thought, and when you observe a thought you can choose whether to keep thinking that thought or let it go.

Overthinking is not fun. Don't beat yourself up about it. We all do it! Meditation is the most effective way to stop overthinking, to check in with yourself, to just BE and not let your thoughts control you and how you feel.

I like to follow guided meditations, they are great for specific things to focus on. For example you can do a meditation for self-love, positivity, a productive day, to cleanse your energy, to calm and many more! There's a meditation to help with everything! So, if there's a specific thing you'd like to meditate to help, just type in that thing with "guided meditation" on YouTube! Or you can just meditate to meditation music and focus on your breath, whichever you prefer!

Also, meditation is not just sitting cross legged and still, meditation can be used throughout your day, by being fully present in the moment, focusing on your breath and your senses, focusing your energy on certain areas of your body, the feeling of water when you are washing your hands, the sounds around you, taking in all of the moment. Every moment of your day can become a meditation by giving all of your focus on what you are doing and how it feels, how your body feels, the pace of your breath, and feeling your heart beat. Realising you are here, now, in the moment and the moment is all there is. The mind takes you away from the present moment, which means you never truly live because your mind is somewhere else. Meditation is basically about becoming one with your inner being and not letting your mind control you. It is a complete life giver. It is the key to just being, your inner peace!

GRATITUDE: Gratitude is so important, always, but especially in the morning! It sets your mood for the day. If you wake up, look at your phone, think about your bad dream or something that happened yesterday, or dread something you are doing today, you are putting yourself in a bad mood, and that is how your day will continue! Gratitude allows us to feel good, to give our focus to what we have instead of what we don't have! Gratitude allows us to attract our dreams because we are grateful for what we already have. If were not grateful for what you already have, what makes you think you'd be happy with more? Appreciate the blessings that you have in your life now, give them your focus! You get more of what you focus on so focus on what makes you feel good and you will attract more of that into your reality! The same goes in the opposite way, so choose wisely! Focusing and giving love and appreciation to the blessings in your life gives you a whole different perspective for life, it gives you a wider appreciation for all things throughout your day. When you come from a place of gratitude, you are even grateful for the bad things that may happen during your day because you are grateful for what they are teaching you. Life is precious, be grateful you are still here! Have an ATTITUDE OF GRATITUDE!

SELF LOVE/AFFIRMATIONS: The words that follow "I am" create your reality. Whatever you constantly affirm, is what becomes real, and is what you believe! Affirmations help you change your beliefs into what you actually want! Look in the mirror every morning and say "I love you, you are amazing!" or something along those lines. No matter how uncomfortable it feels the first few times, keep going, trust me this is very powerful. You will start to believe what you tell yourself every day, so tell yourself how you want to feel! "I am amazing", "I am confident", "I am successful", "I am filled with positive energy", "I attract money in abundance, money comes freely and easily to me", "I believe in myself".

Give yourself LOVE! Thank your body for carrying you, take time to focus on each part of your body and thank it, and give it love! It is the vessel that carries you through this life! Eat a healthy breakfast to fuel the body for the day, fruit is the best thing to eat in the morning. Also, make sure to have a big glass of water when you wake up to hydrate! You must come first! Love yourself at the start of your day, fill yourself up so you can then give to others throughout the day without losing anything from you and draining your energy. This is so important!

MOVE/EXERCISE: Get your body moving in the morning to give you energy for the day and to keep you fit and healthy! Taking care of your body is essential for a great life, health is wealth! Use every day to build your strength and fitness to be the best you can be! You don't have to do a lot, 20 minutes a day is ideal. Get into the habit of doing something every day to keep your body active; go for a walk, do some squats, dance! Just move your body. It may feel uncomfortable but it's worth it, you will feel great once you get into the habit of exercising! Improving yourself is addictive. And so it should be, you depend on your body to get you through life, so keeping it fit and healthy is essential.

LOOK AT YOUR GOALS: To give you motivation for your day, read your goals! You will be more focused and make better decisions in line with what you really want, therefore attracting what you want sooner! For me, looking at my goals gives me purpose and direction for my day. It helps me realise why I'm alive and then I spend my day doing things to get me closer to my goals! Small steps lead to your big goals! Creating a "vision board" is amazing for visualising your dreams, place it somewhere you can see it every day and spend some time really focusing and believing that it's already yours! *Feel* that feeling of already having what you want! Then follow your intuition through the day to guide you to achieving your goals. You will meet certain people, amazing things will happen, just follow your intuition and it will guide you in the right direction!

DO WHAT YOU LOVE: Do something you love, something that makes you happy. Dancing, singing, running, drawing, knitting, whatever it is, just do that! Make sure you are doing what you love every day! Remember this is your life! It is important to enjoy it! So make time to do things you enjoy, and if you do this in the morning it will put you in a great mood for the rest of your day! It is a form of self-love and connection to your purpose. If you do what you love before you take more actions through the day, you will be in an amazing state to do your best with everything else for that day. Doing what you love makes you feel alive!

MOTIVATION: I like to get ready for my day while listening to motivating speakers! What you listen to in the morning is so important, so make sure you are feeding your mind with greatness! Words that make you feel good and stay focused! I love to listen to people shouting at me—in a good way! Pushing yourself is how you grow and listening to successful and empowering people's stories and tips really helps me make great decisions and grow through my day! I listen to this on youtube or Spotify, type in things like "morning motivation" and you will find so many incredible videos!

KNOWLEDGE/READING: Fill your mind with knowledge every day! Every day is an opportunity to grow, to learn more to be better! Read books on subjects that interest you, things that you'd like to learn! For me I mostly read "self-help" books, business books, success books, books that are in line with my dreams/purpose! Books that help me live my best life! My favourite books are **"The Four Agreements" by Don Miguel Ruiz, "Think and Grow Rich" by Napoleon Hill, "Awaken the Giant Within" By Tony Robbins, "The Power of Now" by Eckhart Tolle,** and many more! I have so many books. I wish I could just read them all at once. I make sure I read at least 10-20 pages each day.

PLAN YOUR DAY: Set goals for your day. This allows you to be focused and productive! Write the things you'd like to happen today, imagine the best day you could have and write it down. Write down things that will help you get closer to your goals and make sure you do them. Life goals, yearly goals, monthly goals, weekly goals, and daily goals. All you have are the 24 hours in front of you, just focus on them and use them to get closer to where you want be.

If you find yourself overwhelmed, and there's so much that you want to achieve that you don't know where to start, write down everything you are doing/want to do. Then write in order or importance, and write possible deadlines for each thing, that way you can work out what you need to focus on. Do the most important things first.

LEARN TO FLOW

Don't force things in life, when something doesn't feel right, it isn't right. Learn to follow how you feel and move in that direction. Be at peace with what happens in life, even if it's something you don't like, it has happened for a reason. You can either resist and fight it, which causes more suffering, or accept it and learn to trust the flow of life. When you are feeling good, your intuition is heightened, your intuition is your "inner guidance system". You know, your "gut feeling". This is your guide through life, listen to this always. If you are being sent signs, or you notice something over and over, follow it! Nothing is a coincidence in life. Start to take notice of your path and how everything is connected. It is so exciting when you realise the flow of life and what things you have followed that have led to others! Everything is as it should be. Stay calm, stay in your peace and let life flow.

Then move in the direction the flow takes you, follow what *feels right!*

> **MAGICAL ACTION**—*Write out a morning routine for yourself, and stick it somewhere you will see it every day! Plan each night what time you will wake up in the morning, and when you wake, tick your list when you have done each thing!*

YOU CREATE
YOUR REALITY

Life doesn't just happen to you, life is your creation. Life happens *for* you, life happens *because* of you! Everything you do affects your life. You decide how you will experience your time here, every day you have a choice no matter how small, of how you choose to live.

The most powerful ways you create your reality, which most people don't realise, is through the WORDS you speak, the THOUGHTS you think and then the ACTIONS you take are products of those thoughts and words.

The words you speak and thoughts you think are affirmations. The subconscious mind only says "yes". So if you say "I'm so broke" you are affirming that yes, you are broke, and you'll continue to think "broke" thoughts, and speak "broke" words therefore that is what you will experience.

Do you ever think to yourself, why am I constantly feeling the same way? Why am I constantly broke, or why am I constantly tired, or sick, or whatever shitty things that keep showing up in your life? Whether you realise it or not, you are creating it! It's time to give up on blaming others, and take responsibility for your own life. You are the creator. *You* decide! It takes a second to decide to make a change, the "hard" part is keeping it going. You can decide to not let anything outside of you affect you anymore, stay persistent and you will see results!

Eliminate the thoughts and words that are making you small, which are holding you back from being your greatest and living your best life. CHOOSE thoughts and words that are uplifting, hopeful and positive.

Words and thoughts create how you FEEL, and how you feel is what creates your reality. When you feel bad, you have a bad day. When you feel good, you ATTRACT good!

Your beliefs are habits, and you can change them! It is a choice what to think, even though it doesn't feel like it because you may have thought the same way your whole life. Your thinking won't change overnight, but when you consciously decide to change and *think happy thoughts* then that will become your new habit.

You know what kind of thoughts you are thinking by how you FEEL. How are you feeling right now?

If you are feeling any negative emotions, this is because you are thinking negative thoughts! To feel better, think a better feeling thought. Think about what makes you feel good. Love, appreciation, gratitude, happy memories, think of good things you would like to have happen in the future.

Your future is created by the words you use now. When you choose to say "I am prosperous", you may not have any money in your bank account. You are planting seeds for future prosperity, every time you affirm it, it is growing. When you feel happy, your positive thoughts and affirmations grow quicker, a.k.a come into your reality sooner.

When things are going "bad" in your life and you feel bad, and negative thoughts start to arise, catch yourself before they grow. State "All is well!", "Everything is working out for me", and "I am learning and growing through this situation"

Whenever I feel unwell, instead of focusing on how sick I feel and giving my energy to that, I will give my focus to something that makes me feel good, I will affirm that I feel good! If you feel sick, and you don't shut up about it. You moan and groan and feel sorry for yourself, you are giving more energy to the sickness and you will just feel even more sick! Instead of focusing on problems, give energy to solutions, give energy to how you *want* to feel, rather than how you do feel.

I know for me, when I feel bad, sometimes I can be stubborn and stick to that feeling. My mind is telling me this is how I feel and this is how I'm staying. I give it energy and just feel worse. You know how that feels? When you just feel so angry or so down that you are determined to stay that way, you push out your anger on everything around you, you become this shitty feeling that you have allowed to take over you. I know now that if I want to and choose to, I could change my mood instantly. I could laugh at myself for feeling bad instead of beating myself up for it, I could dance to my favourite music, I could give my mum a hug, I have so many options of things that make me feel good that I could choose in that moment rather than choosing to stay in that bad feeling place. You can do this too! You always have a choice.

WORDS

You know the phrase "If you don't have something nice to say, don't say it at all"?

Well, it couldn't be more true. Not just because its unkind or you could hurt someone's feelings, but because your words actually CREATE your reality. Thoughts create the momentum, which then create the words and words are already a physical manifestation of sound vibration, so they literally become part of your world and shape what happens. Think about an argument, it's not fun energy right? Compare that to a conversation with someone expressing how much you love them. Being conscious with your word choice is essential for living a more deliberate life. You can CHOOSE the words that come from your mouth. Only speak what you wish to create. The word is your power. Words are like spells, hence why it's called "spelling". Gossip is the worst use of the word, it's like black magic. Using your words to speak against others is speaking against yourself, and a complete misuse of your power. It will only bring bad! Use your power of the word for good, to speak positivity; peace, hope, love, encouragement, inspiration, gratitude, appreciation, INTENTION. The words you speak the most are the words you start to believe. Tell yourself a lie over and over, and you'll start to believe it. Hence why you may believe bad things about yourself, it's because you've told yourself that over and over. Change your words to compliment and appreciate yourself! Be conscious of how you speak to others, and of the phrases you use every day. Speak of appreciation!

We all know how that conversation goes "Oh, I'm fine". "The weathers shit isn't it?" "Oh did you hear about such and such . . . ?" "Oh that happened again . . . " Why do people just have a conversation and moan? What is the point in having a conversation at all if that's how you use your words? It's because it has become a habit for people to speak like that, to meet each other and talk about what's wrong in their lives, what's wrong in the world, instead of focusing on what's right. How much better would it be if people met each other and spoke about their blessings? Their celebrations? You have the power to choose your focus. Focus on the good, talk about the good, encourage others to talk about the good.

If someone speaks to you and it feels negative, turn the conversation around! You don't have to go along with their complaining.

I don't know how many times I used to just entertain people gossiping to me or moaning, when I really wanted to say how uncomfortable it made me and could we please talk about something positive? I would just go along with the conversation and be absolutely drained afterwards! Words are energy. Every time you have a conversation with someone, you are exchanging energy. It affects how you feel. Really think about the truth of that. Think about a negative conversation you've had, how did it make you feel? Now think about how a positive conversation makes you feel.

YOU HAVE THE CHOICE

Speak about your dreams/goals as if they already exist! Speak positively every day, speak about what you appreciate! Even when your head is telling you to moan, you have the power to speak positively!

Every time you go to speak a negative statement, consciously stop yourself and speak the opposite, speak what you want into existence!

When I feel shit, I always speak about how good I feel and then imagine feeling those feelings. We have the power to change our state with what we focus on!

Your words are powerful, remember this next time you speak.

THOUGHTS

"The mind is everything, what you think, you become"—Buddha

Your mind is constantly chatting to you, replaying videos in your head from the past or imagining the future. Thoughts can destroy you, or make you feel amazing. You take your power back when you realise that you are in control of your thoughts. It's when you let your thoughts control you that you can be in a bad state.

You are reading this right now probably with your voice in your head saying the words, and you are also listening to that voice. What I mean by this is, you are not your thoughts, you are the observer of the thoughts. You are consciousness above the thoughts, you can exist without your thoughts, but thoughts cannot exist without your attention to them. When you realise this, thoughts can no longer control you, you can consciously control them. When you consciously control and choose your thoughts, that's when you create your reality.

This is because thoughts create feelings, and feelings are how we live. Feelings determine whether we are enjoying life or not, and usually they come from a thought. Even when there is an action that has upset you, it's your thoughts about that action that make you suffer.

Every thought in your head is like a seed, and you can either plant flowers or weeds, that's up to you.

The thoughts you think create your reality. But don't let that scare you, because we can all think negative thoughts sometimes, I know I do! But now I realise they can't control me. I can take back my power and choose not to dwell on them or let them affect me.

So what do you do if you have negative thoughts? Changing the thought from a negative to a positive automatically just is not possible. So, don't put pressure on yourself to do that. Instead, to change your thoughts, focus on your feelings, do something that makes you feel good, then think about something that makes you happy. Focus on that for as long as you can, blocking out everything else. Whether that's thinking about your pet, a happy memory, a place where you feel good, anything! As long as it's something that makes you feel good. You will then start to think happier thoughts.

I like to do something called 'pattern interruption', when I am feeling in a negative place and overthinking, I'll just suddenly start silly dancing, or just laugh. Like literally laugh at yourself! Don't get annoyed because you thought something that didn't make you feel good, just laugh! Like "ha! I said I wouldn't think about that and here I am thinking about it!". Lighten the mood, don't take your thoughts too seriously.

Don't spend any time thinking about what you don't want, for example, "I hate when this happens" or "why is this happening again?" or "I really don't want that to happen" and then thinking about what you don't want, because you're trying to prepare yourself for "the worst case scenario" or something! Realise when you do that, you are actually creating that scenario. Instead, think of a situation that you'd like to happen, think of people you'd like to meet, think of a place you'd like to be. Think about what you want, not what you don't want. Whatever you think about, gives it more power! ENERGY FLOWS WHERE ATTENTION GOES. So if you think about how much you don't want something, you are actually giving it more power! Instead, think about the opposite. Give all of your focus and energy and feeling to that. Think about what you'd like to happen and really feel it.

It's your feelings that matter. Thoughts matter because they create feelings. Think about the things that you want, why do you want them? You want them because of the feelings they will bring! How you will feel when you have them?Feel that now. You can experience what you want now, by choosing to feel that way. That is what will bring what you want to you faster.

We attract what we give attention to. If you focus on the magical, amazing, beautiful parts of life, it is what you will receive more of! If you focus on the problems in life, the stress, the bills, the bad things in the world, that's what you'll experience more of. We always have a choice of what to focus on, and what we focus on is what we experience.

ACTIONS

So, we can't just speak positive words and think positive thoughts and then sit on our ass and wait for life to be amazing, it just doesn't work like that! We need to take inspired actions, from our words and thoughts. Take positive actions that compliment your positive words and thoughts.

If your words are "I am successful", then take actions that a successful person takes. If your words are "I am healthy", then take healthy actions, and eat health, life giving foods— fruits and vegetables, and exercise daily.

You have to take actions every day to live the life you want to live. Put into place everything you learn, make changes, and make progress. Keep moving forward.

Make sure you have a purpose, actions without an end goal, a purpose, are pointless! Your actions are inspired and focused, when you know what the end goal you want to achieve is! You then take actions that are in line with what you want to achieve. You take small actions and big actions every day and before you know it, you're there.

You just have to DO IT! Stop procrastinating and getting distracted. Just do it like tomorrow will never come! You probably, like me, have often said "ah I'll start tomorrow", "I'll do that tomorrow", "I'll do that one day", and then never do it, or go through the same process again weeks, months or years later. You could have just done it when you thought about it. Make a decision and act on it, there and then! "There is no time like the present" as they say.

Your goals are not going to come to you any sooner, by you saying "one day" then just sitting on the couch and watching TV. Creating your best life requires you actually taking action. Remember why you are taking the action, stay focused on what you want to achieve. You will grow, determination will grow. Just DO! You have everything to gain.

> **MAGICAL ACTION**—*Get into the daily habit of thinking before you speak and only speaking what you want to create. Observe your thoughts and think better feeling thoughts. Take daily inspired action!*

GO YOUR OWN WAY

I have always known what I want to do with my life, I have always had huge dreams and a definite vision. I have always known my purpose and known I am meant for great things. I never wanted to settle for an "average" life!

People would tell me, **'You'll never make it'** ,**'You won't do it, it's not possible'**, and make fun or laugh when I told them my goals and what I wanted to do with my life.

For me, settling for an average life that you didn't really want or care about made no sense. **I've always wanted a life that sets my soul on fire.** Passion, depth, purpose, **being** alive. You know why? Because we create our reality. I'm serious! Your life and your decisions and visions for your life are up to YOU. No one else can live your life for you.

I always knew I was destined for something great, and I believe we all are. That's why I get so frustrated when people would give up on their dreams, or think they were just for the 'lucky ones'. Everywhere I see people settling, people pleasing, listening to others instead of their own soul and just following the crowd. These decisions of not following your own path and just doing the "norm", are based on

FEAR, we all know this life is temporary, so why are we not making the most of it? TRULY LIVING. Being the greatest we can be. Fear doesn't have to hold you back, yes it may be scary to walk your own path, but I think it's much scarier to die having never actually lived, to die having never lived YOUR OWN LIFE. Regret is much scarier than having the courage to go after what you want, regardless of what anyone says or thinks.

I left school just before I turned 16, I couldn't wait to leave so I could follow my dreams. I didn't believe in anything I was taught, it always felt so wrong to me. I basically fell asleep in most classes, I didn't really try for any of my exams except business. I knew my grades wouldn't matter for what I wanted to do with my life. I went to college after school, I wasn't confident in myself enough yet to follow my music dreams, so I chose following my fashion dreams. The fashion course was full so I did jewellery but I wasn't passionate about that so I failed the course. Then I saw a music course was opening and I knew that's what I've always wanted the most so I joined.

I got so much from the course, but as I was a teenager that thought I knew everything, I wasn't humble enough to actually learn what is important to know when you are a musician. I just wanted to perform all of the time, and didn't want to learn Music Theory, etc. because it just reminded me of school again. Taking exams to test what I've always known is my passion and purpose felt wrong. I feel the same way now about the schooling system, however if I was to do my music course all over again I would have listened and learned absolutely everything to be the greatest I can be.

But my head was in the clouds, I was distracted by boys and trying to fit in.

I then quit that course halfway through the second year, and learned Make-Up Artistry in Illamasqua, London, after my mum suggested it to me, to add a service to her business. I absolutely loved being able to let my creativity loose, and with my interest in fashion I felt make-up was a perfect fit to getting into the fashion industry. I also love that Illamasqua spreads the message of being true to yourself, being creative, individual and beautiful as you are! The message resonated with me.

However, I totally lost my passion for make-up because I knew it wasn't what I truly wanted. I worked for my mum in her successful Permanent Cosmetics business for around 6/7 years. I was so thankful for the job, the pay was great, I was always able to travel and buy what I wanted, which I am so thankful for. But I never felt passionate about what I was doing as a job, I am a creative person, and sitting on a reception desk didn't allow me to be who I truly was. I tried to leave many times and never did because of the money I earned and I didn't want to let my mum down. However, everything happens as it should and looking back I know why I wasn't ready to leave and follow my dreams, the many times I wanted to.

The most powerful realisation I have had in life is that I don't have to do what others do, or what others tell me to do. You don't have to live the life your parents want you to live, your teachers, your friends or anyone else. You are here to live YOUR life! You don't have to accept what others tell you as truth, you decide what to believe, you decide your path!

You don't have to experience life the way you have been told to, especially by society! It seems like everyone is doing the same thing, but are they really happy? Everywhere around you people are settling. Settling for their jobs, their partners, their life. Seeing life as a planned out system—go to school, go to college or university, get a job, find a partner, settle down, have some kids, get married, then die. If that makes you happy, then great. But for me, an average life, just to follow what everyone else does, is not truly living.

I had life "all set out for me", my mum has a successful business and EVERYONE expected me to carry it on, except my mum—she just wanted me to do whatever made me happy. She did, however, offer to train me in her craft, which could have possibly earned me a lot of money. I would have carried on my mums business that was already set up and successful, and life would have been easy! Every time I met someone that was a client of her business, or a family friend, they would say "Oh Leah, are you gonna be following in your mum's footsteps then?" AND IT PISSED ME OFF SO MUCH! It just got so old, I was sick of everyone expecting me to be my mum! I am not her, my mum was blessed with her own talents and I was blessed with mine. I knew from a very young age that I wanted to be a famous singer, fashion designer. I wanted to be an artist and someone who made a difference in the world. So when people expected me to give that up and live my mum's life "that was already set out for me" it made me so angry! I just didn't understand that perspective of life.

It got to a point where I could no longer work in my mums business, I had no passion, I was becoming bad at my job because I couldn't give my all, and it was time to leave. So I quit my job to follow my dreams!

I was involved in a music project for around a year and a half. We had plans to tour, get a record contract, etc., but something just never fully felt right to me. But I thought, it's an opportunity and I'd be silly to pass up an opportunity, what's meant to be will be. So I followed it. Signs kept showing me that it wasn't right, I knew by the way I felt, my soul was saying no and my head was saying yes. I didn't feel passionate about what I was singing about, I didn't feel the music. Music is such an important thing for me, it is who I am. I need to believe in what I am singing about, and sending the message I want to send to the world. **This is my life, I need to be true to myself.** So I quit, and felt a huge weight was lifted. It was an opportunity people would dream of, but I knew I wasn't being true to myself by following it and I've learned that is the most important thing in this life.

ALWAYS FOLLOW YOUR HEART.

Your purpose has to be lived with PASSION. If you're not passionate about something, how can you make other people passionate about it? How can you make a difference in other people's lives if you're not happy?

Your passions are your gifts, and your purpose is to use your gifts to help others.

With my music, I want to make people feel the way I feel when I listen to my favourite artist. Escapism, connection, emotion, I want my music to make people feel alive. **The greats have the greatest music because you can feel it's from their soul.** They are being true to themselves and pouring themselves into the music. That is special. That is **MAGIC.** I have accepted that my music will happen in divine time, I always thought there was a certain order my life was supposed to happen in, and now I am just letting it flow! It turns out this book, and my clothing, has happened before my music. I always thought I had to be a singer first, then I could do fashion, then I could write a book and help others. I have learned not to resist the natural flow of life, I know it is working out the way it should and I feel so blessed for the dreams I have achieved so far.

So going back to when I left the music project, here I was, no job, no plans. But I never felt better and surer that I was on my true path. Everything has been flowing since then. **You just have to BELIEVE IN YOURSELF, and focus on living your dreams EVERYDAY.** That's what brings them to you. **What you focus on is what you create.**

There is no "right" or "wrong" way to live, there is only YOUR PATH.

Following your soul and what feels right to you is the way. We are all here to live our own truths and our paths are all different. So why would you let someone else tell you how to live your life when they are not you?

"I'm the one that has to die when it's time for me to die. So let me live my life the way I want to."—Jimi Hendrix (one of my biggest inspirations)

It's not going to be easy to go your own way. You will have people questioning you, criticising you, and likely they will be your family and the people closest to you. Change will shock people, because most people don't. Go your own way anyway! You are here to live your life. If they love you they will support you with whatever makes you happy. The only way you are ever going to be truly happy and satisfied is if you live a life true to yourself. All of the answers are within you, not outside of you. There is a reason you love the things you love and want the things you want for your life. You must listen to your true hearts desires, and follow them!

STOP CARING ABOUT WHAT OTHERS THINK

So, there are around 7 BILLION people on planet Earth. We don't even know this for a fact unless we went around counting every single person, which A), would probably take longer than our whole life and B), people are always dying and being born. So, yeah, the point is THERE ARE A LOT OF PEOPLE ON THIS PLANET.

Every single person has a different perspective of life, their own opinions, their own beliefs of what is true and false, right and wrong. I could see the sky as blue, but you could see it as green. We are the only person who sees life from our perspective.

As much as it would be lovely for everyone in the world to love us, like us or agree with us, it is literally IMPOSSIBLE. We are not for everyone and that's okay! You could be the greatest person on Earth, the kindest, most loving, giving and caring person and someone would still say 'Ugh have you seen him/her being so nice to everyone? They are too kind, I don't like them.'

People will always have opinions, and so they should; we all have our own voice.

Let people talk!

You stay focused on YOU!

Nothing is personal in life. Everything others say or do is a reflection of their perspective of life. Never take anything personally, it will save a lot of unnecessary suffering!

Even compliments, they are great of course, who doesn't like to receive a compliment? But I have learned not to take them personally either.

Someone could be having a really great day and say something kind to me. The very next day that same person could be having the worst day ever and say something mean to me, as a reflection of their suffering. If I took this person's compliment personally I would get attached, and the next day when that same person said something completely different, I would suffer. I would think 'Wait a second they liked me yesterday? What's wrong with me today? What have I done?' and end up overthinking about why they said something mean to me. When really, it was only because of something that happened to them, or something going on in their minds. People project their reality upon you, it has nothing to do with you, and everything to do with them.

Take a moment to think of all the people's opinions that you care about, or that bother you and affect how you live. If you died right now, how many of those people would be at your funeral? Probably not many, if any, right? So, why do we give so much of a fuck what other people think of us? One day we are going to die, and so are they. SO LIVE FOR YOU! Do the things that make YOU happy. The people that are meant to join you on your journey of life will join you when you are being true to yourself. If you are not being true to yourself, the wrong people will surround you and make you feel shit for a decision you make if they don't like it.

There will ALWAYS be haters, naysayers, or negative people in the world. Especially if you want to do something out of the norm, or something amazing that others have made themselves believe is impossible for them. If people don't succeed, they naturally don't want to see others succeed and will do everything they can to bring others down, as a projection of their own failures or disappointments. Don't let the haters bother you. Thank the haters. They are what keep us grounded, and keep us hungry for our goals. Let the haters fuel your fire instead of putting it out. Let them build a determination inside of you to prove YOU CAN DO IT! Not just to prove them wrong but to prove that THEY CAN DO IT TOO! That's why I've never let haters stop me from following my dreams, because I want to show them that we can ALL do ANYTHING, we just need to believe in ourselves and stay true to ourselves. We were all destined to live a great life. Shining your light guides others to their own.

I can hear people right now, in the future when I release this book saying, 'Who does she think she is writing a book?' YUP, I see you! You're reading this aren't you? Good. Because I want you to live your best life too, and I send you LOVE!

I have had many people put me down throughout my life. From people in school, teachers, friends, family, people online. It used to hurt me so much, but now I realise it has nothing to do with me. Everything I do is from my heart and with pure intentions and if someone doesn't like it, that's their problem, not mine. I stay true to me! I actually see having people doubt you, or try to make you feel small, as you doing something right. Your standing up for something and that bothers people. When you want to do something with your life, you will always have an opposing force, so prepare for that by no longer giving a fuck what others say/ think.

Practise responding to negativity, hate and criticism with love and kindness. As sad as it is, some people will just never want to see others happy or successful. That is not anything to do with you. Your success reminds them of their failure and their misery. When someone is happy, vibrating higher, people of low vibration will come to try and bring them down to their level, to make them feel better about being negative and miserable. Stay in your peace, stay in your happiness, stay in your success! Don't let anyone ever bring you down; Let your light shine so fucking bright! Rise above the negativity. If you let negative people bring you down, then you're both just going to be negative and not doing anything with your lives and what good is that for anyone? Shining bright may piss people off, but it only pisses them off because they wish they could do the same! And they can. They've just forgotten that. But the only way to help negative people IS to shine! Shining, being happy, being successful, and living your best life inspires others to do the same. It gives them hope! You're reading this book aren't you? If I let people dull my shine this book would never be in your hands and I believe this book has the potential to change your life. It is through me shining my light, which is guiding you to yours!

I used to let other people's opinions affect what I do. I just wanted everyone to like me, everyone to know I'm a good, kind and nice person. I would change myself and people *still* didn't like me! You know why? Because most people don't even like or love themselves, so it's impossible for them to like you! YOU HAVE TO LOVE YOU!

Your life is up to YOU, no one can live it for you. If you like yourself and stay true to yourself, it doesn't matter what other people think. You know you are doing what's right for you. We are all on our own paths here and the only path you can walk is your own. We will never be satisfied living someone else's idea of life.

I could easily let people's opinions stop me from doing what I want to do. But what would be the point of that? You wouldn't be reading this book if I let other people's opinions affect me!

Are we really going to get to our last moments on Earth and think 'Wow, thank goodness I lived my life doing what other people told me to do?'

ARE. WE. FUCK.

"There is only one way to avoid criticism, do nothing, say nothing and be nothing"—Aristotle

We want to get to the end of our lives and say we lived the greatest life we could. We actually did all of the things we said we were going to do, we actually made a difference in the world by following our dreams. We had a great time on this planet with amazing people around us that encouraged us!

If you're worried about losing people in your life, don't be. People are sometimes in our lives for a temporary amount of time because they are only compatible with an old version of you. We're here to grow and growing brings change, so it's natural that you may not get along with the same people you got along with in school, a few years ago, or even a few months ago. If you decide to make changes in your life to be true to yourself and be happy, and someone doesn't like it, makes you feel guilty or whatever. Then that person isn't meant to be on your journey with you. Surround yourself with those on a similar path, people who will encourage, uplift and inspire you. Yes, you may end up alone for a while, but trust me = when you follow your path, your true friends soon appear to join you.

Actually, I think being alone is essential in life. Even if you have a partner, make sure you get alone time every day, just to check in with yourself and make sure you are okay and you are still following your own dreams. Although you are spending your life with someone else, you are still an individual, with your own life and dreams. If you don't have a partner, make the most of being alone. Get to know yourself and love your own company, then you will truly know if someone is meant for you, because being with them will feel better than being alone. You have be happy alone FIRST! Relying on others for happiness only leads to disappointment, because like I said, everyone changes, and sometimes in different directions. Someone may love you today and change their minds tomorrow, and if you don't love yourself first, you will resent them for leaving you and feel broken and unloved. Whereas if you love yourself FIRST, there is no loss if someone leaves you, you understand they are on their journey, and if you truly love someone you will just be happy if they are happy, even if it's not with you.

STOP COMPARING YOURSELF TO OTHERS

ESPECIALLY celebrities.

I feel like celebrities are seen as super human, seen as above normal people and seen as 'somebody'. This creates a false perception like your life isn't worth anything and their lives are because they are famous. You are constantly surrounded by advertising, magazines, products, etc., to make you feel like you are not good enough as you are. Companies prey on our insecurities and use celebrities that we look up to, to sell us a product that we don't need but they make us think we need. We see photo shopped, 'perfect' looking people on magazines and on television, etc. It makes me very sad that in these times it is almost frowned upon to be comfortable in your own skin.

Everywhere we turn there are celebrities, advertisements, comments, and judgements that we need to look perfect and even when people seek this and do everything to change themselves they are still judged for it. It seems like we are never enough as we are. It makes no sense! Absolutely EVERYONE has faults but they make us human, no one is perfect and we never will be. We are only going to be this person for this life, so shouldn't we embrace it and love who we are? If we love who we are, we can truly love others too, and appreciate another's beauty or success, because we are confident and happy within ourselves. You don't have to be like a celebrity to be accepted, you don't have to look like them, wear what they wear or do anything they do. YOU ARE YOU! And that is so beautiful. The most beautiful person you can be is YOURSELF. Someone who fully loves who they are SHINES, and that is why a lot of celebrities are idolized, because they are confident in their skin. You can do the same. Embrace and love who YOU are, flaws included! Your imperfections are perfect.

I used to think being "rich and famous" and societies definition of "beautiful" and having fancy possessions was the ultimate success in life. You couldn't do any better than that, it makes you "somebody" you've "made it". I didn't think I was important until I was going to be "famous" then people would love me and look up to me and treat me as "somebody". That's bullshit! Being rich and famous isn't the answer, it isn't the key to life, to happiness. There are many rich and famous people that are unhappy. True happiness and success can only come from within. I believe true success is being true to yourself, and using your gift, your dreams, your vision, whatever that may be, to make a difference in the world while you are here. You don't have to be famous, or rich, living a full, happy, life full of love and being true to your own soul that is true success.

I used to compare myself to celebrities all the time, wishing I looked like them, wishing I had their lives, their possessions, thinking I would be more important if I copied them, if I saved and bought possessions that a celebrity also had. I would speak about celebrities all the time, follow their lives, I would compare my body to theirs, and feel like shit because I wasn't them. You are you and they are them. We are all souls on a journey as a human for a temporary amount of time, we all have insecurities and fears, and we are all the same. There is no one above or below you, remember that. We are all equal, we are just on our individual paths. Why be a second rate version of someone else, when you could be your own magical, incredible, first-rate self? SHINE AS YOU! You don't have to be rich or famous to be important, you already are important. All you need to do is be YOU!

If, for whatever reason, you find it hard to love yourself as you are right now, find a temporary role model. Instead of being jealous of someone, or comparing yourself to them, think "What is it that I envy or like about this person, why do I wish I was more like them" and take action on that within yourself. In situations think, "What would my role model do?" I encourage having role models if they bring out the greatest version of you. Instead of wanting to be that person, let them INSPIRE you to be the best version of yourself. Until you feel happy just being YOU, then be your own role model!

For me, Slash has helped me a lot in being the best version of myself, I am very attracted to him and admire him as a powerful presence, especially as a performer. Guns n Roses are my all-time favourite band! He has inspired me to bring out my true style, my inner 'badass' and masculine rock star energy. When I am on stage I am a complete extrovert, but in daily life I would play small and be very quiet and soft. I embrace and love my empathic, sensitive, feminine side, which is who I am. I am also that confident, masculine, sensual, badass, powerful energy when I perform. So looking to Slash, my on-stage energy has helped me find a balance and be a greater version of myself, I see myself within him. Whenever I feel like I'm playing small, or feeling anxious especially in social situations, I channel my "Slash energy". So THANK YOU Slash, I will be sending you this book and meeting you one day to thank you in person. So, whoever it is that inspires you, learn from them and allow it to bring out the best version of YOU.

Also, if you have any negative feelings towards someone, i.e jealousy. Change that to LOVE! Support and uplift others, appreciate them instead of being envious! If you see someone and you think they are beautiful, tell them! There needs to be more love and appreciation in the world! Especially between women! As a women I have seen so many women tear each other down, when we should be lifting each other up! We are ALL amazing! Think how much better the world would be if we appreciated and celebrated each other! Don't be scared to give someone a compliment, you could really make someones day! Even a smile can lift someones spirits, smile and appreciate others as much as possible! I have always done this, if in my head I'm saying something kind about someone, I think fuck it why would I keep this in my head when I could potentially make someones day?! So I always say it! There is nothing to lose with being kind!

Choosing to go your own way, choosing to be YOU, is the greatest thing you can do in the world. Know who you are, what your gifts are and use them to serve others. Make your mark on this world, you were here! Going your own way is living the greatest life you can live.

YOUR LIFE IS UP TO YOU AND NO ONE ELSE!

MAGICAL ACTION—*Make a decision every day for YOU and no one else. Even if someone else doesn't like it, if it's right for you, DO IT!*

I Am Free by Leah Luna Lightwarrior

"I know who I'm supposed to be, you can't
tell me nothing about me.
Cause I am free and I am me
And I am being who I was born to be
You can't tell me what's on my mind
'Cause I was told that love is blind
But love is all that sees
And I am free and I am me
So close your eyes and look inside
Go so deep, you'll find the light
Beyond the darkness
Let it flow, don't hold on tight
Be inspired by the night
That's when the stars shine
I am free
I am me."

RE-PROGRAMME YOURSELF

FREE YOUR MIND

The key to changing your life lies within taking back your power of controlling your own mind.

Whether you consciously realise it or not, we are constantly being brainwashed. Brainwashed by our parents, teachers, television, advertising, culture, etc. We are being told how to live and it is becoming a part of our belief system because we are accepting the information. So, you must take back control and *brainwash yourself.*

> **'Whatever we plant in our subconscious mind and nourish with repetition and emotion will one day become a reality'—Earl Nightingale**

The subconscious mind is 30,000 times more powerful than your conscious mind! That's why when you try to change a habit and make the intention in your conscious mind, i.e. going on a diet, it won't work unless you stay persistent, so that it becomes natural, because your subconscious mind will just convince you to eat junk food again.

Your subconscious mind holds your belief systems, and your belief systems control how you live your life! That's why companies spend millions on advertising campaigns, they know the true power of the subconscious mind.

Facts about the subconscious mind:

1. It doesn't understand the word "no" or "not" so if you have the intention "I will not eat junk food" all it hears is "junk food" and that's what you'll think about. Change this to "I will eat healthy foods that benefit my body and wellbeing".

2. It only lives in the NOW. It cannot comprehend the future, it only lives in the present. So if you have something you want to achieve, you have to believe it already is. So, instead of saying "If I become a bestselling author one day", say "I am a bestselling author". Whatever you feed the subconscious mind, it believes and eventually becomes your reality.

3. It picks up everything going on around you, even if you are not consciously aware. If you fall asleep with the TV on or sit in a room and someone next to you is listening to something, it will consume all of the information it hears, it is extremely vulnerable, and this is how subliminal messages work.

You are who you are today, the habits you have, the belief system you follow, who you believe you are, all the labels, etc., because of the subconscious mind. When you were born onto this planet you were pure, full of love and innocent. Then you were taught by others how to live, what life means, who you are, etc. They took control of your subconscious mind, and you took on others' beliefs as your own. I discovered who I truly am when I realised I am not who I've been told to be my whole life. I re-programmed myself and realised I consciously decide what to consume; mind, body and soul. The key to freeing yourself, to living your best life and knowing your true self is by freeing your MIND.

Pretend you are a child again, unlearn and relearn. Recognise the beliefs you have etc., and think did they come from within, or did I take that on from someone else? You FEEL what is right for you. All of the answers are within, nothing is found outside of yourself. When someone tells you something and you feel it is truth, it is because that person is a reflection of you, we are all one. They are reminding you of something you know within. That's why you should always do what FEELS right, not what the mind says.

Realise that you are not your mind, you are not your thoughts. The suffering of humans comes from the mind. It is our minds that tell us negative things, they play movies of worry in our mind, which lives in the past. When we realise that we are not our minds and we can choose to just observe our thoughts and not let them affect us that is when we take back our power. We can truly live in the moment and experience more joy. We cannot stop the mind from thinking, so don't try to. Just realise that you can observe your thoughts and either listen to them or don't. If your mind tells you something negative you can simply thank the thought, laugh at the thought, or just recognise the thought as not your own and let it go.

Your mind is great when used for tasks etc., but it is simply a TOOL. The fact that we can listen to our thoughts shows that we are not the thought, but the consciousness. Consciousness can exist without thought, but thoughts cannot exist without consciousness. So use your mind when you need to, but then let it rest. Live from your soul, from your heart, be present to life! Don't let your mind take you away, you have a choice!

CHANGE YOUR DAILY HABITS

"You will never change your life until you change something you do daily. The secret of success is found in your daily routine."

Your life is determined by what you do every single day. What are your daily habits?

Most of us wake up every morning and do the same thing as the day before. We also think most of the same thoughts and speak most of the same words. It is impossible for you to create change in your life, if you are doing the same things every day. Nothing can change until you change! All it takes is a decision!

There is always a choice of what we do every day, we can make a choice from our lower self (fear) or from our higher self (love, which benefits us and others most).

Make sure your daily habits are actually helping you become a better person and achieve your goals. Switch watching TV to reading books, having a lie in to getting up earlier and exercising, eating junk food to eating plant based foods, listening to the news to listening to empowering speeches. We have limited time on this planet, how you use it matters! Your life is your EVERYDAY.

Every day is an opportunity to grow, to learn more, and to be a better you. We live in a society where people are constantly upgrading their phones, upgrading their cars or whatever. But why are you not upgrading yourself? Every day we can learn something we didn't know the day before, we can gain a new skill, we can choose to make a change to become better. People say to me "How do you not have a T.V, what do you do with your life?!" And I half want to laugh. And my answer is because our time here on Earth is precious, the time a lot of people spend watching T.V programmes, is the time I use to learn, to build my dreams, to truly experience the best life I can. T.V to me is a waste of time. It's a distraction! Some people spend most of their lives in front of that black box that tells them how to live. It's not real, YOU ARE REAL! You are alive right now. You can experience life or you can watch others experience life, it's up to YOU.

Become OBSESSED with "upgrading yourself".

FEED YOUR MIND WITH GROWTH.

CONSCIOUSLY CONSUME

"Whoever controls the media, controls the mind"
—Jim Morrison

To take control of your life, you must take control of what you consume; mind, body and soul.

The information on the media, tells you who to be, what to eat, what to buy, what to believe. You watch other people's lives in envy as if it's not a reality for you because you're watching someone else live it on a screen. Truth is, the time you could spend building that life for yourself, you are using to watch someone else's life. The truth can hurt, but if you are watching people like "The Kardashians" (I use this as an example from seeing how much they influence society—especially woman my age and younger) wishing you had the things they have, you are never ever going to get it by spending your time watching them. Stop consuming the celebrity bullshit, the media is pushing other people's lives upon you like they mean more than yours, you are just consuming products of someone else's life. LIVE YOUR OWN LIFE.

Stop consuming and start CREATING. You are here to live your life and not watch someone else live theirs.

Release yourself from the control of the media, and YOU DECIDE what to consume. You must control yourself or you will be controlled by the outside world. All around us are advertisements, newspapers, TV, all designed to control how you think and live. Most of the things around you are designed to bring you down, i.e. the news. There is a reason they don't tell happy stories; when you are feeling sad (low vibration) you are easier to control. Therefore consume more of what they are selling to you and telling you to believe. You become like putty! YOU ARE YOUR OWN POWER. YOU DECIDE HOW TO LIVE. Stop watching things that bring you down or are not in line with your beliefs and goals for your life, the things you watch have such a huge impact on your life and you don't even realise it! It's more than just "entertainment". There's a reason why it's called television "programming" it literally programmes your mind.

Television is a huge distraction from life. Most people watch around four hours of television per day, over the average adult lifespan that is 13 years of watching TV! Over a decade of life lost. Wasted. TV doesn't make you a better person, it doesn't make you truly happy. It is a distraction! Especially if you are watching junk TV or programmes that bring stress and fear, i.e. the news. If you want to watch TV spend that time watching things that bring value to your life!

LOVE OVER FEAR

Choose to feed your mind with positivity and growth. Every day I watch people who inspire me, whether its musicians like Michael Jackson, or empowering speakers like Tony Robbins. I make sure I only watch/listen to things that benefit me and are in line with my goals and life purpose. Everything not in line with who I am, I consciously ignore. Time on this planet is precious and I care only for growth, knowledge, love, and inspiration. We DO NOT have to listen to or watch the news, we don't have to watch or listen to advertisements or anything else that brings us down, makes us anxious, makes us upset or feel like shit. We can CHOOSE to watch/ listen to things that make us feel empowered. Motivated, inspired, happy!

Simple things like realising you can turn the volume down on your radio when the news comes on, or even a song you don't like. It was so weird when I realised that I used to just listen to adverts or whatever like I didn't have a choice to just turn it off. All of that stuff you don't wanna hear or that makes you feel bad, goes into your subconscious mind and becomes part of your life. The subconscious mind is very powerful and very vulnerable so feed it goodness for it to truly benefit you.

YOU ARE WHAT YOU EAT

It's important to realise you literally become what you eat! Your food tells your body what to do, so you have the choice every day to either feed your body with disease, or health. Food is made to fuel your body, not for pleasure or taste. Realise what we have been told to eat, what surrounds us.

When I found out the truth about our "food" I was horrified. It made no sense that I had spent my life eating animal products and chemicals. Because it's seen as "normal" we are surrounded everyday by unhealthy "food". Being healthy isn't just for losing weight, being healthy is LIFE. HEALTH IS WEALTH. The only way you can live a truly happy and healthy FULL life, is if the body is healthy, and health comes from what we consume! We have a CHOICE.

I used to think "healthy" eating was boring, taking the fun out of life! I thought "Why not just treat yourself to a cheeseburger?!" Not realising WE ARE OUR OWN DOCTORS. The food we eat determines whether we are sick or healthy, that then determines the life we live. If we are feeding our bodies dead, tortured, stressed, suffering animal flesh, what is that telling our bodies to do?

If you were to tell me two years ago that I was going to be a 'Vegan', I wouldn't have believed you! I would have probably laughed at you actually. I remember always saying,

> **'I could never be a Vegetarian! I LOVE meat! I couldn't live without it!'**

> **'I mean WTF do Vegans eat?! Salads? NO THANK YOU!'**

I loved my 'food' too much to give it up. I lived off of fast food burgers, pizzas, and a lot of meat. I thought being a Vegan was some sort of trend, a new diet to lose weight, or just a way to look cool and hipster. Here I am today, as a vegan and animal activist, not only living but **THRIVING**, and passionate about making the world a better place.

Like most people, I was conditioned to believe that eating animals and drinking their milk was 'normal', and what we were supposed to do. **I would give love and appreciation to my beautiful dogs, whilst sitting eating a pig, cow or chicken, and calling myself an 'animal lover'.** Reading that now looks absolutely crazy, but at the time, I didn't think twice about it.

I'd see slaughter videos come up on my Facebook feed and I'd quickly scroll by, I didn't want to see that! **It made me upset and uncomfortable, but yet I didn't add up the fact that I was actually PAYING for this to happen, and then eating the flesh of the animal that had been killed.**

Ignorance is bliss, right?

I would eat these animals, not realising the effect it has on your body. I believe everything is energy, and when an animal's life has been taken (animals don't voluntarily let you eat them) they suffer. They are scared, they feel pain. They have gone through a great deal of trauma to get to your plate, you are then consuming that trauma. It truly has an effect on your body! You are feeding your body death, suffering, and bad energy! I used to think it tasted so good, but really if we were meant to eat animals, we would eat them raw! We would hunt and tear them apart with our teeth. Can you really imagine seeing an animal and thinking "MMMM YUM, I want to eat you!" And proceeding to chase it down and tear it apart? Definitely not! It's not natural. We have PETS! We LOVE animals! If it's not natural for us to eat our dog or cat, it's not natural for us to eat ANY animal! They are all beautiful beings filled with love, they feel, just like us!

You know yourself, if you have pets, they are the sweetest, purest, most beautiful beings that give unconditional love and look to you to protect them and love them. They make our lives amazing and give us happiness! They are part of our family. Your dog is the same as a pig, a cow, a chicken, a sheep, or any other animal we have been conditioned to see as food. We see bacon, 'sausage, beef, etc., instead of seeing what it REALLY is, and that is an animal that wanted to live.

When did we determine which animals we love and which we kill?

And then think about milk. Our bodies do not need milk to survive, the only milk we need is our mother's breastmilk. Just like baby cows need their mother's milk. We are the only species that drink the milk of another species, how weird is that? What need does the human body have for cow's milk?

You are probably thinking WHY right now. Why are we told eating animals and drinking their milk is normal. Why is it advertised constantly? Well I would highly recommend watching 'What The Health' on Netflix for the answer to that question.

I believe being 'Vegan' is our natural state of being. If you are reading this and you have not made the choice to go Vegan, I would really encourage you to watch documentaries, do some research, but most importantly look to your own heart for the truth. Within you, you know what's right. You don't have to go Vegan right away, it can be a process. Start by cutting down on your meat intake, switch to oat, almond, or coconut milk instead of cow's milk. Small changes can make the biggest difference. Even things like 'Meatless Mondays', but I guarantee you once you educate yourself, you won't want to eat it at all!

We are living in the age of information, and many people are now realising the truth about how eating animal products affects our health and the planet, and of course the animals. Many people each day are switching to a plant based diet, there are so many amazing documentaries out there so there is no reason to hide from the truth anymore! Make the best decision for your health, the animals and the planet! We can be and will be the generation that SAVES THE PLANET! Basically, it's time to give a shit.

MAGICAL ACTION—*Write a list of your daily habits and see which ones make you feel good and which ones don't, replace the ones that don't with new ones. Do these new habits every day for 21 days to become a part of your natural habits! Make the morning routine one of them!*

GIVE, NOT TO RECEIVE

The language of the soul is love, giving, kindness, and connection. Connect with your soul to truly FEEL ALIVE. Without a doubt the best feeling in the world is GIVING. Whenever you feel down, give to someone else, someone who really needs help and couldn't give to you in return. Feel the incredible gift of giving happiness to another. Guaranteed whenever you feel shit and like life isn't worth living, try giving to someone else, and then see what it really feels like to live with purpose. To live from a place of selflessness. Kindness is UNITY. We are all on this planet together, why not help each other? Lift each other up, make life easier for each other. Life feels so much better when we connect with others in a genuine, loving way. We are stronger together! There are so many labels in society that separate us, realise that beyond all of the labels, we are all the same. We are souls living a temporary human life. We are all on our own journeys, but we are here together and essentially even though we are on different journeys, we experience the same things. Life can be tough and we don't know what someone else is going through. Be kind always! We all have the power to make someone's day, to make life easier and happier for someone else by an act of kindness. Live from the heart. The heart is powerful.

Listen to the heart over the mind. The heart is what makes you human, what connects you to everyone else. To feel compassion, empathy for another. Everyone is you! Take away my name, my race, and nationality and anything you believe keeps me separate from you, and then what am I, I am you. Deep within we are all the same, all equal.

PRACTISE KINDNESS

"The world is filled with kind people, if you can't find one, be one."

Be one anyway! You lose nothing from being kind, and gain everything! A sense of purpose, pure magic and joy! The world needs more kind people and it starts with you! Consciously choose to be more kind , choose kindness in situations, to choose love! Practise responding to criticism with kindness and love. The power of choosing love is not allowing negativity to take over you. Not taking things personally, and understanding that person is maybe being unkind because of their own problems, it has nothing to do with you! If someone insults you, breathe, smile, say "Thank You", stand in kindness! You will definitely shock some people! "An eye for an eye makes the whole world blind" but responding with kindness is healing the world! It's being the change you wish to see, and making the world a better place just by that simple choice to be kind. And it feels so freaking GOOD!

Give your time to others, especially those that cannot give in return. Giving to someone just to get something back from it is not truly giving. Let go of expectation and just give purely because you can and you choose to! You choose to help another.

CONNECT WITH NATURE

Nature isn't separate from us, it is who we are, and we belong to nature just like every other creature on this planet. Look at the branches of a tree, they are like our veins, trees give us oxygen, they keep us ALIVE! If possible, connect to nature daily, walk in the fresh air, appreciate the beauty of the planet, and hug a tree! I'm not kidding!

I literally used to hate going into nature! My mum used to drag me on walks and I would complain just wishing I was going shopping or to the cinema or something! I thought nature was boring and for old people or geeks! So crazy!

Now, nature is my savior, my happy place, my feeling of peace. Whenever the world feels like it's getting too much, I remember who I am in nature. Nothing else matters, I'm truly in the moment when I'm in nature. Nature is REAL. It wasn't created by man, it is LIFE. We are life. For us to live our best lives, we have to remember what we are a part of. Ground yourself in nature, go barefoot and feel the electrons. Charge yourself on the soil. FEEL ALIVE! A lot of us live in cities, with manmade houses, manmade businesses, and people walking around like robots going to work! It can get to be too much! I believe this isn't the way we are meant to live. Without humans, the planet would be filled with beautiful nature, untouched; we are meant to be a part of nature! Nature is part of the higher power, whatever you believe that to be. We are also part of the higher power, therefore nature is a part of us!

CONNECT WITH ANIMALS

Animals communicate in unconditional love. To give to an animal is true giving, they can only give you love in return. A connection with an animal is truly the most rewarding connection, that's why so many people have pets and get so attached to them! They give pure unconditional love, they just ask for basic needs and love! That's it! No expectations, no judgements, just pure LOVE! When you give love to an animal they will give you the most beautiful love in return. Spend time with animals as much as possible, learn from them, give them love, and just BE with them!

"Until one has loved an animal, a part of one's soul remains unawakened."—Anatole France

Planet Earth Is Our Home

So, I don't know if you've realised but we're actually on a planet right now. A huge, beautiful planet with many beautiful things to see and interact with. So many places to see and parts of Earth to experience! All of this planet is our home! You are not defined by where you were born, you are an Earthling! Staying in one place your whole life is like never leaving your bedroom! Explore the planet while you are here! Experience as much of it as you possibly can! We never know if we are coming back here or not! Travelling is truly living! Go where your heart wants you to go, you do not have to stay in the same place no matter what anyone says! Don't ever live in fear! Embrace the unknown. Live your adventure, experience everywhere in the world, learn grow and evolve from all the different people and places you see. Life shouldn't be lived in one place!

We also have a responsibility to take care of our planet, it's the only home we've got! Just like you clean your house and make it comfortable for you to live in, it's even more important that we look after our planet! Our time here is short, but our impact lasts forever! What kind of planet do you want to leave behind? Every decision you make every day, affects the planet. Every purchase you make, determines what kind of world you want to see. Every single person on this planet has an effect.

Simple things, such as when you see litter, pick it up! It may not be yours but we all have to take responsibility in looking after the planet, we must be an example for others! If you see someone littering, politely and kindly inform them of the effect that it has on the planet! So many people live in an "I don't give a fuck" mindset, and just do whatever they like here and that is why the planet is the way it is now. We must be the change!

Treat animals better, humans better, ourselves better, and the planet better.

Have love and care for our home planet Earth.

Be the generation that saves the planet!

> **MAGICAL ACTION**—*Make a habit of doing at least one kind thing for another being and the planet every day!*

LOVE CONQUERS ALL BY
LEAH LUNA LIGHTWARRIOR

"The world needs love, the world is cruel
They try to trick me, but I'm no fool
The world needs peace, the world has pain
All here to play this crazy game
This is life, it has a meaning
It hurts to see so little people who believe it
This is life, what are we here for
To love and care for one another
But we all want more
The world needs patience, no time for hatred
Don't fight over possessions that aren't needed
Why are there countries, why are there borders?
Separated from each other, so there is war
This is life, how do we see it?
We all long for something more than just breathing
This is life, it happens to us all
How do you choose to live it, will you rise or fall?
LOVE CONQUERS ALL."

FOLLOW YOUR DREAMS

There is nothing more painful than regret, than an unfulfilled dream that could have been.

We've all said "someday I'll do this" or "someday I'll do that", well you are here NOW "Someday" is TODAY.

Tomorrow isn't guaranteed, DO IT NOW! Make the decision today to start working towards your goals.

The only thing stopping you is YOU.

It's time to give up blame and excuses. Outside circumstances or outside opinions can only affect you if you let them. You have the power to choose not to let anything stop you from living the life you deserve. No matter what your circumstances, you CAN succeed. You are not defined by your past, by your struggle. We ALL struggle. It's all part of life. Life isn't meant to be easy, we are here to grow. Life would be boring if it was easy and everything we wanted was just handed to us. The hard times build character, they build strength. They teach us and help us grow as a person and have a new perspective of life. They are like gold coins we collect along the way, like in a video game, there will be obstacles but you have to keep going to grab the "gold coins". Rewards come after challenges in the form of lessons. So failure isn't even a thing! You can only fail if you don't try. Never, ever give up on your dreams.

Some of the most successful people in the world had the toughest beginnings, and have failed many times on their way to their success. Oprah Winfrey grew up in poverty, had an abusive childhood and was fired for being "unfit for TV", she is now a billionaire and one of the most influential people in the world. Marilyn Monroe was dropped by 20th Century Fox for not being "pretty or talented enough" and she is now known as one of the most beautiful women of all time, an icon. Albert Einstein was thought to be mentally challenged and told he'd "never amount to anything" and we all know him as a legendary genius! Anyone who has ever done something great in the world, has failed more times that most people have even tried! If they can do it, SO CAN YOU.

Realise that the greats that inspire the world every day, aren't super human or special. They are no different from you and me. They have just made the most of themselves and used every day to grow and fulfil their true potential. We ALL have limitless potential within us, it is your choice whether you use it or not.

Most people give up on their dreams, or don't even try. They believe the "good life" is for the "lucky ones". Instead of living their dreams, they settle for a life less than they are truly capable of living. A life that's "average", average relationships, average income, average career, average health . . .

If you are working a job that you don't feel passionate about, living pay check to pay check, you are not truly living, you are just existing. What is the point in just existing, when you could experience truly living? Those people you see "living the life" aren't just "lucky". They have believed in themselves and didn't give up until they achieved their goals. *You can do that too.* It requires change, it requires persistence, and it requires determination. You must stay FOCUSED on your goals, don't let anything stop you!

Don't let yourself settle, it's NEVER TOO LATE, or too early, to chase your dreams.

Most people are so afraid of failing that they never even try, there is no such thing as failure. The only way you can fail is by not trying, because you're letting yourself down and you're letting the world down. Your gifts are your purpose in this world, and they are needed! You were born to be GREAT, not to be "average". You weren't born to pay bills and die. You were born to SHINE. Don't be afraid of standing out, be afraid of living an average life. Let failure be your motivation, let failure be your teacher. Every failure is a lesson, grow from that and find another way. Make your goals so big that you can't achieve them until you BECOME THE PERSON THAT CAN. You become your greatest self by going through all the shit life throws at you and making it out of the other side stronger and wiser than before.

THE PATH TO SUCCESS IS A PATH OF FAILING, AND GETTING BACK UP AND TRYING AGAIN AND AGAIN UNTIL YOU SUCCEED.

PERSISTENCE IS KEY.

We ALL have goals for life! It doesn't necessarily have to be, to be rich, or famous, or travel the world, or be the inventor of a world changing product.

Success is whatever it means for YOU.

Success is HAPPINESS.

It doesn't matter how much money you have, how many worldly possessions, fancy clothes and cars. If you are not happy, then what's the point? Happiness comes from WITHIN. It comes from being true to yourself and doing what you love!

What would make you feel truly happy and fulfilled, that you would know you truly lived your life and did what you wanted to do?

Decide what it is you want from life. You know truly what you want, just somewhere along the line you may have stopped believing that it's possible. Realise now that ANYTHING is possible. It starts with believing!

Your purpose in life is found within the things that LIGHT YOU UP. Your gifts, your talents, you passions. FOLLOW THEM! You have them for a reason!

When you are doing what you love, everything else comes naturally. You'll make money more easily because it will flow to you. If you focus on money, you worry about money and you give money the wrong type of energy and instead of attracting it, you wonder why it doesn't come to you, and it's a whole stressful circle. Whereas if you're making money doing what you love, the money is a bonus. You will be happy, enjoying your life and that is when money flows to you easily! Don't make money your focus, if you do something just for the money you will be unhappy! Would you rather do what you love, or work a job you hate just because you get paid for it? You could work so hard for money but then you never even get to do anything with the money or enjoy any of your life because you are too busy working. There is no passion in that kind of life, there is no fulfilment in working for someone else's dreams when you could be working on your own. If you don't follow your own dreams, you'll get paid to work for someone else's.

"The meaning of life is to find your gift. The purpose of life is to give it away"—Pablo Picasso

The world needs you to follow your dreams! That is your purpose here, which is your contribution to the planet. Your gifts are needed now more than ever, it's time to use them, and it's time to do what you love! When you shine your light you guide others to shining their own. Just imagine how amazing the world would be if we were doing what we loved and sharing it with each other.

Gifts are not just singing, dancing, sports, etc., you could have a gift for cutting hair, A gift for growing vegetables, a gift for cooking! We were ALL given a gift! Focus on that gift and become the best hairdresser you can be, the best vegetable grower, the best cook! Gifts come in all different forms, because we are all unique! What's your gift? What do you love to do more than anything else? DO THAT!

All of us want to live our greatest life, within our careers, our health, our relationships, none of us want average! However most people accept average because they don't believe they can achieve more, or just don't believe they deserve it. We ALL deserve to live our best lives and we are all *capable* of living our best lives. Settling is a choice. We always have a choice, no matter the circumstances, you do what you BELIEVE you can!

CHOOSE TO BELIEVE IN YOURSELF.

You have nothing to lose and EVERYTHING TO GAIN!

Imagine life was to be taken from you right now in this very moment. You would never get to come back to Earth again, you wouldn't see the people you love again. Your life is done. How does that feel? What do you wish you would have done? What would be your regrets? THAT IS HOW YOU SHOULD LIVE!

Get a pen and paper and just write down EVERYTHING that you want from life. **DO NOT LIMIT YOURSELF**. Imagine you are a child, let your imagination run wild!

Don't focus on what IS and base your goals around your current situation, just write what you want your life to be.

Then make all your notes into a bullet point list, giving as much detail as you can, and write your goals in the PRESENT, as if they have already came into reality i.e.,

'I have an incredible job as a _____ that I feel truly passionate about. I look forward to working every day because I am doing what I love'

'I am a successful writer, my books have sold millions worldwide and helped many people change their lives.'

'I travel the world and meet new people and experience beautiful moments.'

This is a very powerful exercise. It may seem silly or too simple to make a difference, but even just by writing your goals, you bring them into physical existence. It is an intention then, it has moved from your head.

Do this for every area of your life; career, living environment, relationships/friendships, spiritually, health and fitness . . . Decide what it is you want in each area of your life. You want to live the best possible life in EVERY area, not just an amazing career but your relationship is shitty, or an amazing relationship but your health could be improved. Aim for the best in every area of your life!

Take actions every day towards making your goals a reality. Don't freak out too much about the bigger goals, make small goals and celebrate every win along the way! Focus on the 24 hours and you using them to get closer to where you want to be. Sometimes looking at your main goals can make them feel too big and too far away, and you may lose focus or drive because you start to believe it's not possible. So that's why it's important to take it day by day, and make smaller goals. Every small goal is a step on the path to your dreams.

"You don't have to see the whole staircase, just take the first step".

Dreams will remain just dreams unless they turn into goals. Then the goals turn into plans, and the plans turn into actions.

GET OUT OF YOUR COMFORT ZONE.

> *TAKE RISKS, JUMP. SAY YES TO OPPORTUNITIES, MAKE DECISIONS, tomorrow never comes do it now!*

To follow your dreams you must have the courage to take a risk. That is how greatness is achieved, trust in your journey. Let go of fear; to do this we must conquer our fears one by one. BE GREAT.

Never see mistakes or failures, there are only lessons. Every person, every experience, is there to teach us. Grow from the setbacks, trust the detours. Everything happens for a reason and in the right time. Just keep trusting, keep moving forward, and learn from EVERYTHING.

> LET GO

> When you hold onto the past, you are not allowing new things to flow to you. You must release the past to move forward. This could be past situations, relationships, possessions, etc.

CLEAR YOUR LIFE.

Release all that no longer serves you and your dreams. This may be painful but it allows you to grow. Thank the past and everything it taught you, but now it is time to move forward.

The past no longer exists, there is no reason to still live there. **Every day is a new day and a new opportunity to grow.**

TRUST THE PROCESS

Do not focus on 'how' you will get to your dreams. Know your end result and focus on that. Your dream can come into your life in many different ways, so do not get attached to a particular job, or opportunity, or partner. Be open to how your dreams will come to you, just keep moving forward.

Trust in your intuition to guide you to meet the right people, situations, etc., that will bring your dreams into your reality. Whenever you get an instinct to do something, or go somewhere, follow it! Take action on your instincts.

When you manifest your dreams, you have to meet the Universe halfway, by taking action and moving forward. Your intuition is your inner guidance to take you in the right direction.

ACT AS IF

I know you will have heard the term "fake it 'til you make it", well it's so true, but it's more like 'BELIEVE IT TO RECEIVE IT'.

If you talk about your dreams not being here and believe they are not going to happen, then they won't! Act as if you already live your dreams now. Act as if they are your reality, speak about them as if it already is, think about them as if it already is, and make plans like you have already achieved your goals. Know without a doubt in your mind that they are yours. You must BELIEVE! Even though you can't see them right now, you must know in every part of you that you have them already, they are just waiting for you to get them and become the person to receive them. Believe you already have them now, visualise and feel. Talk to your friends and family about them like it already is. Don't say words like "if only", say "I HAVE" and "I AM". Affirm you already have your goals. BELIEVE BELIEVE BELIEVE!

If you had your dreams right now, what would you be doing, saying, wearing, how would you be acting?

Recreate yourself into the person you want to be. Act as if you are this person until you are. **IMAGINE THE GREATEST VERSION OF YOURSELF POSSIBLE, THAT'S WHO YOUR TRULY ARE.**

The more you feel like you are living your dreams now, the quicker they will be pulled into your reality. Prepare for them to arrive!

For example if you dream of meeting a lover, take yourself on dates, buy an extra toothbrush, and leave a space in your bed. If you wish to travel, go on small adventures, take the bus to a random place, explore and try new things! Doing these things attract new feelings which attract your dreams.

STAY INSPIRED

A positive mindset is ESSENTIAL for attracting your dreams.

Listen to motivational speakers and read inspiring books. The difference these simple things make in your perspective is incredible.

What we read, listen to, watch, all goes into our subconscious mind, which affects our reality and creates our everyday habits. You are in control of what you feed your subconscious mind, so choose to watch, read and listen to things that are in line with your dreams.

Have a mentor, even if it's someone you don't know or is not necessarily with you in person, i.e. someone you look up to with similar gifts, a 'hero' of yours. Know that if they can do it, so can you! Take inspiration from them to remind you of your goals.

CREATE A VISION BOARD

A board of pictures and words that reflect your goals and the life you want to live. Cut out scraps of the place you want to live, the places you want to travel to, the car you want, etc. And look at it EVERYDAY! Vision boards are so powerful. Put it somewhere where you will always see it, to keep you motivated.Remember to always keep your words in the PRESENT tense when writing your goals

I AM AND I HAVE . . .

FIND YOUR WHY

This is the most important part. This is what will keep you going when things get hard. Who could you help by following your dreams? What would you receive and achieve? Your why must be bigger and stronger than your fears and doubts. Your why is your fuel. Maybe you want to get your goals to provide a better life for your family, to make a difference in the world, to leave a legacy. Your why is essential to your success, stay focused on that and keep going! You will get there!

ENJOY YOUR JOURNEY

Since beginning my spiritual journey, following my purpose and finding who I truly am, I have experienced many indescribable magical times and also very hard, dark, painful times. Life seems like a roller coaster of **'ups'** and **'downs'**, **'bad times'** and **'good times'.** Life isn't all sunshine and rainbows, as much as we wish it were. But even if it was, it would probably get boring, how would we grow? How would we learn? But why is it that everything can't just be easy and the good times last?

When you feel down/depressed/anxious, it can be so tempting to want to stay there; to get comfortable in the pain, feeling sorry for yourself and making others feel sorry for you. Now, I recognise that when I'm feeling down or depressed I am being shown something, it is an opportunity to grow because we can choose to not feel like that anymore and get to the root of what is making us feel that way. Realise YOU always have the power to choose how you feel. When I feel down I literally FORCE myself to do something such as exercise, dance, or listen to music because that makes me feel good. Do something creative! Suffering comes from the mind, so when we distract the mind we can feel good! We get what we focus on so the more energy we give to our negative thoughts the more they grow and become negative feelings and you just feel like shit! The more you think about how shit you feel, the more shit you will feel. You are giving this more power by giving it your attention. We have the power to change everything by how we feel, and a change in how we feel can be experienced in an instant. Do what brings you joy, it is not possible to feel sadness and happiness at the same time!

Everything in life is temporary, the good times don't last, but neither do the bad!

Why must we suffer? A lot of the time you will find suffering comes from our **MIND**. We create our own suffering through the perspective of the experience. If you are identifying an experience as 'good' or 'bad' you are determining how you feel. A change in perspective can make the 'dark times' in our lives the most rewarding times. As difficult as it feels, the dark times are **ESSENTIAL** for our time here on Earth. We are here to learn, to evolve, and to grow. If everything was easy all of the time, what would be the point of life?

There is no such thing as an 'easy' or 'perfect' life, EVERYONE experiences hard times no matter what their circumstances. **We are all one and equal** beyond all of the illusions of separation. We all experience the same things just in different ways, we are all on different paths and everyone's path has challenges.

So how do we use these dark times to help us grow instead of feeling like all is lost and giving up?

ACKNOWLEDGE HOW YOU FEEL

The first and most important step to healing is to honour how you feel.

We've all been there; 'I'm fine' and 'Nothing's wrong', although I encourage **focusing on the positive** and speaking positive words. Denying your feelings is different. It is essential to **RELEASE,** whether that's speaking out loud to yourself, speaking to a loved one or writing down how you feel. This takes a huge weight from our minds and allows us to move forward to find a solution

LOOK WITHIN

Healing can only happen from **WITHIN.** Anything outside of yourself will only be temporary to cover up how you feel inside. So forget about buying a new handbag, or getting a new boyfriend. If treating yourself lifts your spirits as a form of **self-love**, then definitely do it. But it is not the solution! This is only avoiding facing yourself, when you should come FIRST. **Knowledge and love of yourself is essential for life.** Don't avoid it. Get to know and love the beautiful, amazing being that you are.**TAKE CARE OF YOURSELF**

It is so important to be kind to YOURSELF. Stop beating yourself up, be kind to yourself, forgive yourself. This is an essential part of healing, blaming yourself and negative self-talk is the worst thing you can do. You will always be YOU! So be kind to yourself, listen to your thoughts to make sure they are beautiful, positive and encouraging! Take some time for yourself, have a relaxing bath, make yourself feel good, treat yourself, read a book, etc., whatever makes you FEEL GOOD! Whatever you do, don't stay in your bed feeling sorry for yourself. Giving yourself love and feeling sorry for yourself are completely different things. As harsh as it sounds, literally force yourself to do things that make you happy, things as simple as listening to your favourite music, watching your favourite movie, or spending time with your best friend! Get into nature, exercise, eat healing foods! (i.e. fruits and vegetables) drink lots of water, stay hydrated! RAISE YOUR VIBRATION!

DON'T RESIST

Resisting something and thinking about how much you don't want it, actually gives it **MORE POWER!** Research the life changing 'Law of attraction'. Switch your focus! You get what you focus on, so **focus on what you want** instead of what you don't want. You hold the power to create your reality, and that power is within your **attention, change your perspective to change your life**. Gratitude is the best way to change your energy, focus on what you are thankful for, we all have something, no matter how small it may seem, **just be grateful you are breathing**! Feel gratitude for every bit of your life. Have an **ATTITUDE OF GRATITUDE.** Life is about balance and contrast will always exist, so think of the contrast as showing you what you don't want, therefore showing you to give more energy to what you do want!

LOOK FOR THE LESSON

In my experience since my spiritual awakening, I have had many times of darkness. I now realise these times of darkness and depression are **healing** times that allowed me to **EVOLVE**. Every time I have felt low and felt like giving up, I have experienced breakthroughs that have allowed me to move forward. I have had so many of these experiences that I look at myself over the months and truly see how much I've evolved. Every time I heal, I get closer to my truest and greatest self in order to live my true life purpose.

Take a step back and try to understand what you are being taught from this experience. What feelings are coming up for you that don't feel good?

Write down how you feel so that you can look at it and realise what needs healing. Most of the time it leads back to **self-love**! A book I highly recommend is called 'The Mastery of Love' by Don Miguel Ruiz. It truly helped me love myself and stop looking outside of myself for love or approval and it enabled me to understand life more.

Now that I realise what's happening, it's like being in a video game and picking up the clues to get to the next level. My 'higher self' tells me the message and then it's up to me to act on it! No action means no result! Sometimes I go through the same lessons over and over until I take action on them and move forward. You will find this happening through life, we will be sent the same lesson in many different ways until we learn.

It can feel so tempting and comfortable to stay in that dark place and feel sorry for yourself, but you **MUST** keep moving **FORWARD**! Do things that make you happy. Push yourself through to **LEARN** and that's when you'll get your breakthrough and BAM! You've evolved. And you'll keep leaning and growing, and that's the beautiful thing about life. We can never stop **GROWING**!

TRANSFORM THE PAIN

We can always turn our pain into something BEAUTIFUL. Positive actions can replace negative thoughts. Do something creative with how you feel, write a poem or a song, play your favourite music and dance the pain out, or go for a run and take out your pain on a good workout. Either way, the pain needs to find a way to leave the body! Don't let it build up inside you, don't let it stay in your head because it will just bring you down deeper. Make the decision that you are a creator and you will use this pain to benefit you. It won't win. The greatest artists in the world use their pain to create beautiful songs or paintings. You don't have to be "good" at creating, there is no good or bad, creativity is great therapy. We are all creative in some way! Your art is an expression of you, no one has to even see it! Do it for yourselfl. There is always going to be pain in life, so decide that you will use it for good! Sadness to frustration is a great step in the right direction because you can then take out that frustration in a positive way, like at the gym! Get angry at the gym and let it all out while making your body stronger! Pain can ALWAYS be turned into a positive.

Every day of life is an opportunity to learn and grow. We are here to evolve, everyday holds an opportunity to be better. Every experience we have here is a lesson. We are never going to be finished or 'complete', there will always be something more to learn or do. That's life! We should be making the most of every moment of our time here.

In my opinion, if someone is the same person at 50, as they are at 30, then they have wasted 20 years of their life. Along my journey so far, I have realised I cannot beat myself up for where I am not, I just always recognise how far I've come. I use every day to become a better me than I was yesterday. I have experienced such growth on my journey to my true self and potential that I feel like I experienced lifetimes worth of growth in just a couple of years, its truly incredible. We *all* have the potential to do this! We all have the potential be a new and improved version of ourselves. Learning from everyone we meet, seeking new knowledge, expanding our mindset, learning new skills. Life is so beautiful because every day is a new adventure, a new experience, we have the opportunity to be new in every moment.

We are here to evolve. If we are not growing, we are dying. All of nature grows, and we are nature.

A beautiful friend who taught me a lot once told me, "If you were given every meal of your whole life at once would you even enjoy it?" If you received all of your goals right now it wouldn't feel the same. It's all about the journey, and even when you get to your goals, you'll have new goals to reach.

Enjoy the journey, that's the best part! We will never reach a final destination, the journey is LIFE. Happiness is now, stop waiting to be happy because you create it in this very moment.

RISE by Leah Luna Lightwarrior
"I show my scars so others know they can heal.
I just wanna show them what's real.
It's not what you see, hear or touch, its what you feel.
So what's the deal, with hiding your emotions?
Just let them all flow, let them all go.
That's the only way to grow.
But don't waste your life crying.
Rise again like fire.
Rise my child, it's alright.
Set your flame alight inside, and light up the night.
If it wasn't for the darkness, you wouldn't see the stars.
So, know your worth dear child,
The world is ours."

This is the beginning of you living your greatest life.

You decide how you experience your time here.

You ARE a fucking unicorn!

ACKNOWLEDGEMENTS

TO THE PEOPLE THAT INSPIRED MY INNER UNICORN

I have a lot of thank yous, as I feel it is so important to give thanks to every soul I've connected with on my journey of life so far, if I haven't thanked you and you have been a part of my life, you will know who you are. I thank you. All of the people I have met and spent time with on my journey here on Earth, whether you blessed my life, or created suffering, I thank you. You made me who I am today, whatever you brought to my life allowed me to learn and grow.

To the people that bullied me in school, I FORGIVE YOU and I TRULY THANK YOU. You gave me the strength and determination to chase my dreams and never give up. I thank 'the haters' for keeping me grounded and allowing me to understand that everyone has their own life and perspective and I can't waste time trying to make people like me. I choose to be me and focus on LOVE.

Most of all I thank the people that believe in me, that encourage me. My mum, who is my best friend in the world and brings out the best in me, you gave me life on this planet and I am so blessed that I get to be your daughter and spend precious, magical time with you. You are my favourite being in all of the universe.

My sister, Madison, thank you for inspiring me every day, thank you for being YOU, I am truly blessed to have you, Pickle, we have each other ALWAYS, you make me laugh and enjoy life and that is a very precious gift.

To my 'auntie' Julie-Anne, I had to give you a special shout out for all of the magic you brought into my life as a child, you truly encouraged me to be who I am and that means more than anything, you will always be my soul family!

To my grandad, thank you for always believing in me, for your words of wisdom and your beautiful spirit that you show to me, you will always be my best friend. To my granny thank you for everything you are the best granny I could ask for, my dad thank you for being you and giving me life I love you, and all of my family for everything you have taught me and given to me, and for just being my family! You all know how much I love you.

My grandpapa and Gran Gran, you have transitioned and you both will always mean so much to me and inspire me every day. I love you and I'll see you in another life. Ad Infinitum.

Rugas you are a dog and can't read this but I don't even care. You are the most special soul I have ever known and words can't describe how much I love you and am thankful that I get to spend time with you on Earth. My babies Hendrix,

Nashii and Yogi. Thank you for showing true unconditional love and bringing joy to my life.

To an extraordinary person in NYC that I met in October 2015. "J" (I'll keep your name secret). Thank you for being you. I have spoken about you in this book because meeting you is what led me to finding myself. I fell so hard in love with you that it put me in a lot of pain, and that pain led me to finding who I truly am and allowed me to RISE and follow my true purpose. We have to come to a place of darkness to find the light, we have to realise we are lost to find ourselves. So thank you for unknowingly putting me in that place so that I could heal. Everyone you meet in this life is for a reason, so I thank you for what I learned from you, and you probably didn't even know it. You will always be special to me and I will always love you. It doesn't have to be reciprocated, I just wanted you to know that I do, life is precious and words from the heart should always be spoken. Thank you. I wish you so much love and happiness in your life. You are meant for great things.

To my supporters and soul family that connect with me online, THANK YOU. I feel so truly blessed to connect to you all every day and share my story. It means more than anything to be able to be a part of your journey. I love and appreciate you all!

I acknowledge the souls that embrace who they truly are and shine their light to guide others to their own. There are so many human beings that inspire me every day to be my truest, greatest self.

MY BIGGEST INSPIRATIONS: The souls that I haven't had a physical connection with, but still inspire me every day!

I first thank the GREATS, the artists that have transitioned from this planet, however still continue to inspire me and remind me of who I am every day and leave an impact on this planet, Jimi Hendrix, Michael Jackson, Prince, Bob Marley, and Amy Winehouse.

Britney Spears, you were my childhood inspiration and you truly remind me of my dreams and the magic I felt looking up to you as a child, thank you for being in my eyes, *the* popstar. Also thank you for taking time out to call me on my 17th birthday, you have no idea how much that meant to me! THANK YOU!

Slash, you inspire me every single day, whenever I feel down I play Guns N Roses and I LIGHT UP. You inspire me to release my inner badass and mesmerise me with your incredible presence and musical gifts, you are a true irreplaceable great. You inspire me to be the best version of me and for that I am truly grateful! You are fucking amazing! Also, thank you for being a voice for the animals, they need us to speak up for them. What you are doing is amazing and ALL animals need our voices, so I ask on behalf of the animals that need your voice, to look into being Vegan and the true cruelty of eating meat and dairy and wearing animal skin. Every one of us can truly make a difference. You are amazing! Thank you for being YOU. Excited to collaborate with you one day!

Pharrell Williams, you have been one of my biggest creative inspirations since childhood, a true magical being. N*E*R*D and your music have helped me through shit times in my life and keep my magic ALIVE. THANK YOU from my heart for being so true to yourself and such a beautiful role model for others. I look forward to the day I get to thank you in person and would be honoured to create with you!

Thank you to these beautiful souls who are a part of my everyday life, whether that's through their art or wisdom, you remind me of who I Am through being you and for that I am truly thankful, KEEP SHINING.

Tony Robbins—THE MAN, the way you light up when helping people truly reminds me of who I am and what I came to this planet to do, and essentially what led me to writing this book, THANK YOU.

Don Miguel Ruiz—The author of books that truly changed my life, my gratitude is infinite.

Abraham (Esther Hicks)—I listen to you nearly every day and you truly remind me of my purpose and connection to the Universe and my true inner power, THANK YOU.

Shane (connecting consciousness on IG)—Your live streams and posts have helped me connect to who I truly am and why I am here, thank you for always being a reminder and sharing your wisdom, I appreciate you so much!

Amun Ra El (@1eternalnature)—King, thank you for dedicating your life to assisting the collective, you truly align me to my higher self by sharing your wisdom, thank you for being a reflection of the higher consciousness, we are ONE.

Kid Cudi—WOW. I cannot wait to thank you in person one day, your album 'Passion, Pain and Demon Slayin' truly makes me in tune with my true self, whenever the outside world is bringing me down and making me feel lost, I play your work of art and feel ALIVE. I actually become the music, the vibrations are so powerful. You bring pure magic to my life. Can't thank you enough for shining your light and sharing your gift with the world. So much love.

Kat Von D—thank you for inspiring me to be my true self and express who I am, to be a BADASS, and most of all for being a voice for the animals. You are a true GODDESS and incredible, beautiful, magical being. You have given the "weirdos" of the world so much freedom to be exactly who we are. Keep being YOU! You fucking rock.

Miley Cyrus—I have felt such a strong connection to you since a young teenager, I remember how much I looked up to you. You truly reminded me of who I was, I even spent some time working as a tribute act! Now I see you as a sister of mine, even though we have never met in the physical. I feel we are on such similar journeys, you are a true FUCKING UNICORN! Thank you for being your magical self and representing the HIPPIES! So much LOVE for you!

Erykah Badu—GODDESS OF LIGHT, THANK YOU. For truly being YOU. US. Using your voice for true wisdom, peace and unity. Your music truly raises my vibration and brings out my true creative energy from The Universe. "A spiritual woman is the greatest threat to the status quo". I STAND WITH YOU QUEEN. We got this! INFINITE GRATITUDE.

Sade—Queen, you are so radiant and words can't express how grateful I am for your music. I can listen to you and instantly feel good! You are an ANGEL.

Stella Santana—I listened to your album "Selfish" every single day in 2017, which was the most powerful year of my life. Your music truly helped me and my mum feel our absolute best. Whenever we wanted to feel good we would automatically say "Put Stella on!" You have a truly beautiful gift Queen and I KNOW we will collaborate one day! I would be honoured! Thank you for sharing your gift with the world and bringing light into my life! Your music raises my vibration, keep creating! I am so excited to follow your career and all of the music you continue to create!

Paris Jackson—Thank you for being YOU. And being a voice for the planet, for peace, for love, for unity. Keep shining your beautiful light!

Kehlani—I am so truly grateful for you. I felt guided to come and see you live even though I hadn't previously listened to your music and I INSTANTLY felt a connection. The message you were sharing to the crowd was so beautiful to see a TRUE role model, you truly reminded me of myself. You are such an inspiration and encouragement for me to follow my purpose, seeing you spread the message of higher consciousness and using your voice for the planet and its beings is FUCKING INCREDIBLE. Thank you for BEING THE CHANGE and being EXACTLY WHO YOU ARE AND CHOOSE TO BE. A true UNICORN. I feel blessed to be on Earth at the same time as you to see you RISE. Thank you Goddess.

Maggie Rogers—wow. What a beautiful bright light you shine to the world. Your music makes me feel truly ALIVE. Thank you for sharing your gifts for Mother Nature and being your true self. It is so beautiful to see. I feel blessed to have discovered your music, it is a true blessing in my life. KEEP SHINING GODDESS!

Martina Gutfriend—thank you for being your magical, beautiful self. You helped me find the magic and me, and lead me to discovering that I AM NATURE. Your page guided me to remembering and I fell truly in love with the forest, which then lead me to remembering more of my truth. I started to express myself more because of you! Your light is so bright, keep creating and being you and I hope our paths align one day and I can thank you in person!

Janet Jackson—you are just, wow. Your performances and music inspires me so much I can't explain. You are INCREDIBLE. A true great. Thank you for blessing the world with your gift.

Willow Smith—SISTAR. You are a beautiful bright shining light. Thank you for using your voice for the collective, raising the vibration, planting the seeds of higher consciousness. We know why we came to this planet! WE GOT THIS! Thank you for being the true YOU.

Baddie Winkle—thank you for being a true embodiment of the fact that age doesn't mean a thing! You are completely true to yourself and it's so inspiring! Keep being fucking magical, you are incredibly inspiring!

Flatbush Zombies—my sister got me into you guys, thank you for spreading higher consciousness, your music and art is incredible and you guys are just so true to yourselves! So amazing to see especially in the industry, you are being the CHANGE! Thank you for sharing your gifts! You're fucking awesome!

Thank you to the guides that pushed me to actually writing this book!

Thank you to **Andy Harrington** for your 'Power To Achieve' event that truly inspired me and allowed me to let go of the things that were holding me back, to follow my greatest life and share my story!

Thank you to **Vishal Morjaria** and Wow Book Camp, without you I wouldn't be actually getting my book done! Thank you for all of your support and the beautiful souls I met in your class, it is a blessing to encourage each other with our books!

Belinda—thank you for teaching me a powerful lesson that allowed me to let go and know my true worth to grow into the true Goddess that I Am, EYE LOVE YOU QUEEN!

Ruth—thank you infinitely for being a very important guide on my journey, I will never forget you, and I feel so blessed that our paths crossed in this life. You truly guided me to my higher self and my truth. Thank you for sharing your wisdom and being your beautiful bright shining loving light! You embody a true GODDESS! I love you!

Magical Mason—you have been such a beautiful and powerful teacher on my journey of life, you and your mum are such magical, amazing beings and I want to be a part of your life to see you grow up! I will always be your best friend, you can count me as your big sister! You are so very special!

To the souls that have been closest to me on my journey before and while I found who I truly am, whether our connection was romantic or friendship, each of you taught me something and I thank you for that. I thank you for the beautiful, special times we shared and I will always treasure them and have love for you and wish you so much love and happiness on your journey of life; Lauren Young, Colleen, Alex, Lauren McMonagle, Kiran, Tilly, Allan Wilson, Cassey, Sharissa, Mahri/Alex, Caroline, Alan Tait, Rob and Louie.

To my soul family, you know who you are. I feel so blessed to connect with you in this life and elevate each other! My soul siSTARS that came into my life as I found who I truly am (and before), thank you for shining your light. I treasure our soul connection, I know we will always be connected no matter where our individual paths take us. Neecy, Amy Walker, Amber, Jade, Clemmie, Melissa, Louise Lil L, Laura Maginess, Jen Cooper, Veronica, Lauran, Carina, Paige, Saisha Starseed, and of course beautiful Danielle who transitioned in 2017, you brought such light to my life even for the short time we met in the physical, I will never forget you.

To my soul brother Edwin, thank you for always supporting me, love you! Nathan and Brad, love you guys, excited to keep supporting each other in making this world a better place. Thank you James English for sending me that video that started my journey and for being a true brother to me,

I am so thankful to you, KEEP SHINING! Barry, thanks for helping me be the greatest I can be, you're awesome!

There's so many people I could thank, I think I would be here forever and have the hugest list of names, and so thank you to everyone I've ever connected with in life. Whether you are still in my life or not, I have love and gratitude for you.

AND THANK YOU TO YOU! FOR READING THIS BOOK! I LOVE AND APPRECIATE YOU!

9 781999 584504